THE

SOUL IS HERE

FOR ITS OWN JOY

Sacred Poems

from Many Cultures

EDITED BY

ROBERT BLY

THE ECCO PRESS

INTRODUCTION AND SELECTION
COPYRIGHT © 1995 BY ROBERT BLY

ALL POEMS NOT IN THE PUBLIC DOMAIN ARE
REPRINTED BY PERMISSION

ALL RIGHTS RESERVED

THE ECCO PRESS
100 WEST BROAD STREET
HOPEWELL, NEW JERSEY 08525

PUBLISHED SIMULTANEOUSLY IN
CANADA BY PENGUIN BOOKS CANADA LTD., ONTARIO

PRINTED IN THE UNITED STATES OF AMERICA

LIBRARY OF CONGRESS
CATALOGING-IN-PUBLICATION DATA

THE SOUL IS HERE FOR ITS OWN JOY :
SACRED POEMS FROM MANY CULTURES /
EDITED BY ROBERT BLY. —1ST ED.
P.   CM.
ISBN 0-88001-355-9
0-88001-475-X (PAPERBACK)
I. RELIGIOUS POETRY.   I. BLY, ROBERT.
PNM6110.R4S68   1995
808.81'9382—DC20   95-16868

THE COPYRIGHT ACKNOWLEDGMENTS ON PAGES 255–261
CONSTITUTE AN EXTENSTION OF THIS PAGE.

DESIGNED BY MARK ARGETSINGER

THE TEXT OF THIS BOOK IS SET IN
MONOTYPE FOURNIER
9 8 7 6 5 4 3

CONTENTS

PART III:

THE QUESTION OF GREED
AND CONSTANT HUNGER

CONTENTS

PART VI:

LOVING GOD THROUGH

LOVING A WOMAN OR A MAN

CONTENTS

PART VIII:

LEAVING THE BODY OR ENTERING IT?

CONTENTS

xiii

Unless otherwise noted, translations are by Robert Bly.

CONTENTS

AN AFRICAN STORY
AS AN INTRODUCTION

Once upon a time there was a man who had about twelve cows, and he loved his cows. Every morning and evening he would praise them for the amount of milk they were giving and praise them for their beauty. One morning he noticed that the amount of milk had lessened. Each day for a week he noticed the same thing. So that night he decided to stay up and see what was going on.

About midnight, he happened to look up at the stars, and he saw one star that seemed to be getting larger. It was—and the light got stronger as the star came closer and closer to earth. It came straight down towards his cow pasture and stopped a few feet from him in the form of a great ball of light. Inside the light there was a luminous woman. As soon as her toes touched the ground, the light disappeared, and she stood there like an ordinary woman.

He said to her, "Are you the one who has been stealing milk from my cows?" "Yes," she said, "my sisters and I like the milk from your cows very much." He said, "You are very beautiful. And I'm glad that you like my cows. And so this is what I want to say: If you marry me, we can live together, and I will never hit you and you won't have to take care of the cows all the time. I'll take care of them part of the time myself. Will you marry me?" She said slowly, "Yes, I will. But there's one condition. I have brought this basket with me, and I want you to agree that you will never look into this basket. You must never look into it, no matter how long we are married. Do you agree to that?" "Oh, I do," he said.

So they were married, and they lived together very well for six or seven months. Then one day, while she was out herding the cows, he happened to notice that basket standing in a corner of the house. He said to himself, "Well, you know, she is my wife, so it could be considered to be *my* basket. After all, this is my house, and the basket is in my house, and so it could be considered *my* basket!" After he had said this, he opened the basket and then began to laugh. "There's nothing in the basket! There's *nothing* in the basket! There's absolutely nothing in the basket! Nothing! There's nothing *in* the basket!" He kept saying these words and laughing so loud that his wife eventually heard the laughter.

She came into the house and she said to him, "Have you opened the basket?" He began laughing again. "I did!" he said. "I opened the basket! There's nothing in it! There's nothing in the basket at all! There's absolutely *nothing* in the basket! Nothing is in the basket!"

She said, "I have to leave now. I have to go back." He cried out, "Don't go! Don't leave me!" She said, "I have to go back now. What I brought with me in the basket was spirit. It's so like human beings to think that spirit is nothing."

And she was gone.

* * *

I had originally intended to name this anthology after this wonderful African story, so that the anthology would be called *Baskets That Hold God.* But I'm not sure we know how to weave baskets that well. I chose instead a line of Rumi that Coleman Barks has beautifully translated. The line, in his words, goes: "The soul is here for its own joy."

I

Starting on the Path

The poems of the first group center around the difficulty of starting on a spiritual path. A meditation teacher who had come from India once gestured to the floor and said to me, "I have initiated so many Americans, so many the last ten years, that a page from each would make a file up to my shoulder. And where are they all? I am very surprised that people would accept initiation without really meaning it."

Some people experience puzzling events as they adopt a path. At the start, everything is better, one sleeps well, people like your face, you have more energy; then suddenly someone steals your car, your landlady kicks you out, your girlfriend or boyfriend leaves, your mother says you have to do the probate work, and you get a low-grade, long-lasting fever. Someone inside has heard about it. Ghalib in this "world of infinite possibilities" had expected to see hundreds of tracks leading into the distance; but: "All I see is one footprint."

We know, too, that sometimes people can come to spiritual work too early; they may stop because they are not ready. Finally, the soul is aware of fear. In that sense, it is we ourselves who wish for the interruption:

And those who leave the town wander a long way off
and many perhaps die on the road.

Those who are left behind "in the town" may feel some anger. Mary Oliver remarks:

The Footprint

GHALIB

In this world of infinite possibility
I look around for the second step
of desire—
All I see is one footprint!

Sunset

RAINER MARIA RILKE

Slowly the west reaches for clothes of new colors
which it passes to a row of ancient trees.
You look, and soon these two worlds both leave you,
one part climbs toward heaven, one sinks to earth,

leaving you, not really belonging to either,
not so hopelessly dark as that house that is silent,
not so unswervingly given to the eternal as that thing
that turns to a star each night and climbs—

leaving you (it is impossible to untangle the threads)
your own life, timid and standing high and growing,
so that, sometimes blocked in, sometimes reaching out,
one moment your life is a stone in you, and the next, a star.

The Name

TOMAS TRANSTRÖMER

I got sleepy while driving and pulled in under a tree at the side of the road. Rolled up in the back seat and went to sleep. How long? Hours. Darkness had come.

All of a sudden I was awake, and didn't know who I was. I'm fully conscious, but that doesn't help. Where am I? WHO am I? I am something that has just woken up in a back seat, throwing itself around in panic like a cat in a gunnysack. Who am I?

After a long while my life comes back to me. My name comes to me like an angel. Outside the castle walls there is a trumpet blast (as in the *Leonora Overture*) and the footsteps that will save me come quickly quickly down the long staircase. It's me coming! It's me!

But it is impossible to forget the fifteen-second battle in the hell of nothingness, a few feet from a major highway where the cars slip past with their lights dimmed.

We thirst at first

EMILY DICKINSON

We thirst at first—'tis nature's act—
And later, when we die,
A little water supplicate
Of fingers going by.

It intimates the finer want
Whose adequate supply
Is that great water in the west
Termed Immortality.

from *Like to the Arctic Needle*

FRANCIS QUARLES

Like to the arctic needle, that doth guide
  The wand'ring shade by his magnetic pow'r,
And leaves his silken gnomon to decide
  The question of the controverted hour,
First frantics up and down from side to side,
    And restless beats his crystal'd iv'ry case,
    With vain impatience jets from place to place,
And seeks the bosom of his frozen bride;
    At length he slacks his motion, and doth rest
His trembling point at his bright pole's beloved breast.

E'en so my soul, being hurried here and there,
  By ev'ry object that presents delight,
Fain would be settled, but she knows not where;
  She likes at morning what she loathes at night:
She bows to honour; then she lends an ear
    To that sweet swan-like voice of dying pleasure,
    Then tumbles in the scatter'd heaps of treasure;
Now flatter'd with false hope, now foil'd with fear.
    Thus finding all the world's delight to be
But empty toys, good God, she points alone to thee. . . .

This Cloud

DOGEN

This slowly drifting cloud is pitiful;
what dreamwalkers men become.
Awakened, I hear the one true thing—
Black rain on the roof of Fukakusa temple.

Lord, you called

ANONYMOUS 14TH-CENTURY ENGLISH POEM

Lord, you called to me,
And I did only answer thee
With words slow and sleepy:
"Wait a while! Wait a little!"
But while and while have no end,
And wait a little is a long road.

In this town

RAINER MARIA RILKE

In this town the last house stands
as lonely as if it were the last house in the world.

The highway, which the tiny town is not able to stop,
slowly goes deeper out into the night.

The tiny town is only a passing-over place,
worried and afraid, between two huge spaces—
a path running past houses instead of a bridge.

And those who leave the town wander a long way off
and many perhaps die on the road.

A remembrance is moving
JUAN RAMÓN JIMÉNEZ

A remembrance is moving
down the long memory, disturbing
the dry leaves with its delicate feet.

—Behind, the house is empty.
On ahead, highways
going on to other places, solitary highways,
stretched out.
And the rain is like weeping eyes,
as if the eternal moment were going blind—.

Even though the house is quiet and shut,
even though I am not in it, I am in it.
And . . . good-bye, you who are walking
without turning your head!

The Scattered Congregation
TOMAS TRANSTRÖMER

1

We got ready and showed our home.
The visitor thought: you live well.
The slum must be inside you.

2

Inside the church, pillars and vaulting
white as plaster, like the cast
around the broken arm of faith.

3

Inside the church there's a begging bowl
that slowly lifts from the floor
and floats along the pews.

4

But the church bells have gone underground.
They're hanging in the drainage pipes.
Whenever we take a step, they ring.

5

Nicodemus the sleepwalker is on his way
to the Address. Who's got the Address?
Don't know. But that's where we're going.

Friend, it's time

ANSARI

Friend, it's time to make an effort,
So you become a grown human being,
And go out picking jewels
Of feeling for others.
Through the help of holy men,
And the good that comes from waiting on them,
Hopefully your cheeks will grow pale,
And your enthusiasm for exciting life
Will get paler and paler.

A Voice

WILLIAM BUTLER YEATS

One day I was walking over a bit of marshy ground close to Inchy Wood when I felt, all of a sudden, and only for a second, an emotion which I said to myself was the root of Christian mysticism. There had swept over me a sense of weakness, of dependence on a great personal Being somewhere far off yet near at hand. No thought of mine had prepared me for this emotion, for I had been pre-occupied with Aengus and Edain, and with Manannan, Son of the Sea. That night I awoke lying upon my back and hearing a voice speaking above me and saying, "No human soul is like any other human soul, and therefore the love of God for any human soul is infinite, for no other soul can satisfy the same need in God." A few nights after this I awoke to see the loveliest people I have ever seen. A young man and a young girl dressed in olive-green raiment, cut like old Greek raiment, were standing at my bedside. I looked at the girl and noticed that her dress was gathered about her neck into a kind of chain, or perhaps into some kind of stiff embroidery which represented ivy-leaves. But what filled me with wonder was the miraculous mildness of her face. There are no such faces now. It was beautiful as few faces are beautiful, but it had not, one would think, the light that is in desire or in hope or in fear or in speculation. It was peaceful like the faces of animals, or like mountain pools at evening, so peaceful that it was a little sad. I thought for a moment that she might be the beloved of Aengus, but how could that hunted, alluring, happy, immortal wretch have a face like this?

Maybe

MARY OLIVER

Sweet Jesus, talking
    his melancholy madness,
        stood up in the boat
            and the sea lay down,

silky and sorry.
    So everybody was saved
        that night.
            But you know how it is

when something
    different crosses
        the threshold—the uncles
            mutter together,

the women walk away,
    the young brother begins
        to sharpen his knife.
            Nobody knows what the soul is.

It comes and goes
    like the wind over the water—
        sometimes, for days,
            you don't think of it.

Maybe, after the sermon,
    after the multitude was fed,
        one or two of them felt
            the soul slip forth

like a tremor of pure sunlight,
  before exhaustion,
    that wants to swallow everything,
      gripped their bones and left them

miserable and sleepy,
  as they are now, forgetting
    how the wind tore at the sails
      before he rose and talked to it—

tender and luminous and demanding
  as he always was—
    a thousand times more frightening
      than the killer sea.

As kingfishers catch fire
GERARD MANLEY HOPKINS

As kingfishers catch fire, dragonflies draw flame;
  As tumbled over rim in roundy wells
  Stones ring; like each tucked string tells, each hung bell's
Bow swung finds tongue to fling out broad its name;
Each mortal thing does one thing and the same:
  Deals out that being indoors each one dwells;
  Selves—goes itself; *myself* it speaks and spells,
Crying *What I do is me: for that I came.*

I say more! the just man justices;
Keeps grace; that keeps all his goings graces;
acts in god's eye what in god's eye he is—
Christ. For Christ plays in ten thousand places
Lovely in limbs, and lovely in eyes not his
To the Father through the features of men's faces.

Written on a Monastery Wall

LI SHANG-YIN

They rejected life to seek the Way. Their footprints are be-
fore us.

They offered up their brains, ripped up their bodies; so firm
was their resolution.

See it as large, and a millet grain cheats us of the universe:

See it as small, and the world can hide in a pinpoint.

The oyster before its womb fills thinks of the new cassia;

The amber, when it first sets, remembers a former pine.

If we trust the true and sure words written on Indian leaves

We will hear all past and future in one stroke of the temple
bell.

Translated by A. C. Graham

Our journey had advanced
EMILY DICKINSON

Our journey had advanced,
Our feet were almost come
To that odd fork in being's road,
Eternity by term.

Our pace took sudden awe,
Our feet reluctant led;
Before were cities, but between,
The forest of the dead.

Retreat was out of hope;
Behind, a sealed route,
Eternity's white flag before,
And God at every gate.

The Starlight Night
GERARD MANLEY HOPKINS

Look at the stars! look, look up at the skies!
  O look at all the fire-folk sitting in the air!
  The bright boroughs, the circle-citadels there!
Down in dim woods the diamond delves! the elves'-eyes!
The grey lawns cold where gold, where quickgold lies!
  Wind-beat whitebeam! airy abeles set on a flare!
  Flake-doves sent floating forth at a farmyard scare!—
Ah well! it is all a purchase, all is a prize.

Buy then! bid then!—What?—Prayer, patience, alms, vows.
Look, look: a May-mess, like on orchard boughs!
  Look! March-bloom, like on mealed-with-yellow sallows!
These are indeed the barn; withindoors house
The shocks. This piece-bright paling shuts the spouse
  Christ home, Christ and his mother and all his hallows.

Sometimes a man

RAINER MARIA RILKE

Sometimes a man stands up during supper
and walks outdoors, and keeps on walking,
because of a church that stands somewhere in the East.

And his children say blessings on him as if he were dead.

And another man, who remains inside his own house,
dies there, inside the dishes and in the glasses,
so that his children have to go far out into the world
toward that same church, which he forgot.

Rainbow at Night

ANTONIO MACHADO

For Don Ramón del Valle-Inclán

The train moves through the Guadarrama
one night on the way to Madrid.
The moon and the fog create
high up a rainbow.
Oh April moon, so calm,
driving the white clouds!

The mother holds her boy
sleeping on her lap.
The boy sleeps, and nevertheless
sees the green fields outside,
and trees lit up by sun,
and the golden butterflies.

The mother, her forehead dark
between a day gone and a day to come,
sees a fire nearly out
and an oven with spiders.

There's a traveler mad with grief,
no doubt seeing odd things;
he talks to himself, and when he looks
wipes us out with his look.

I remember fields under snow,
and pine trees of other mountains.

And you, Lord, through whom we all
have eyes, and who sees souls,
tell us if we all one
day will see your face.

II

Longing for the Garden

Religious life usually began, in the Middle Ages, with the entry into privacy. The Garden, when it is thought of religiously or inwardly, is feminine in tone; it is a place of precious plants, cultivated, guarded by walls, where one feels safe enough to become a pear tree or a rose bush or turn into a fountain that pours out water in four directions. One can be safe enough, as Lalla says in this second section, to dance naked. In the true Garden, one is dancing in the presence of God only. Gerard Manley Hopkins, when he wrote his Garden poem, spoke as if he were a woman, a nun taking the veil:

> I have desired to go
>   Where springs not fail,
> To fields where flies no sharp and sided hail
>   And a few lilies blow.

So safety is a strong part of the Garden. It is a place where the soul can "withdraw into its happiness"; the soul can fly up to the pear tree, and there, as Marvell says, "it sits and sings, / Then whets and combs its silver wings."

We recognize that the manger, protected by cows and sheep, was a sort of Garden—a place where "the soul is wound into the body":

> If you could turn your heart
> into a cowstall,
> Christ would be born again on earth!

A poem is a kind of Garden, Rilke says, if the writer manages to resolve a hundred contradictions into a single image. For Blake, the Garden of Eden was also a Garden where ears heard "The Holy Word / That walked among the ancient trees." The Holy Word is "Calling the lapsed soul." Antonio Machado speaks so beautifully of the sorrow, "the aloneness of the soul in shadow." In George Herbert's poem, God says that if a human being can't come through goodness, "weariness / May toss him to my breast."

Finally, looked at in a certain way, the whole world, which the Sufis call an orchard, is a Garden, and God is the one invited in:

Come to the orchard in Spring.
There is light and wine, and sweethearts in the pomegranate
    flowers.
If you do not come, these do not matter.
If you do come, these do not matter.

Heaven-Haven
A nun takes the veil

GERARD MANLEY HOPKINS

I have desired to go
　　Where springs not fail,
To fields where flies no sharp and sided hail
　　And a few lilies blow.

And I have asked to be
　　Where no storms come,
Where the green swell is in the havens dumb,
　　And out of the swing of the sea.

LONGING FOR THE GARDEN

from *The Garden*

ANDREW MARVELL

What wondrous life is this I lead!
Ripe apples drop about my head;
The luscious clusters of the vine
Upon my mouth do crush their wine;
The nectarine and curious peach
Into my hands themselves do reach;
Stumbling on melons, as I pass,
Ensnared with flowers, I fall on grass.

Meanwhile the mind from pleasure less
Withdraws into its happiness;
The mind, that ocean where each kind
Does straight its own resemblance find;
Yet it creates, transcending these,
Far other worlds and other seas,
Annihilating all that's made
To a green thought in a green shade.

Here at the fountain's sliding foot,
Or at some fruit-tree's mossy root,
Casting the body's vest aside,
My soul into the boughs does glide:
There, like a bird, it sits and sings,
Then whets and combs its silver wings,
And, till prepared for longer flight,
Waves in its plumes the various light.

Is my soul asleep?

ANTONIO MACHADO

Is my soul asleep?
Have those beehives that work
in the night stopped? And the water-
wheel of thought, is it
going around now, cups
empty, carrying only shadows?

No, my soul is not asleep.
It is awake, wide awake.
It neither sleeps nor dreams, but watches,
its eyes wide open
far-off things, and listens
at the shores of the great silence.

The Dweller

ROBERT BLY

There is a dweller in the dark cabin.
Who is this, someone hearing and telling?
The relative has come, the dark ocean shell.
This is something solid, a dweller in the dark cabin.

The face of the cabin awakens—
What the savage loves in his madness.
The cavern itself wakes up. There is a traveller—
He has to be awake—sleeping in the cabin.

Far down in my dream, I dreamt a bearded fish,
An old one, immense, slipped into my arms.
The traveller gone so long has returned.
There is a dweller in the dark cabin.

The linen merchants find Joseph singing.
Small grains of thread join into longer strings,
Indistinguishable from music when they join,
Something mingling, continual, eternal.

Who is that? A man travels here and there,
Something slowly gains solidity in November air.
Our relative from the lair and the shell has come.
There is a dweller in the dark cabin.

If you could turn your heart

ANGELIUS SILESIUS

If you could turn your heart
into a cowstall,
Christ would be born again on earth!

O God Our Help in Ages Past

ISAAC WATTS

1

O God, our help in ages past,
  Our hope for years to come,
Our shelter from the stormy blast,
  And our eternal home.

2

Under the shadow of thy throne
  Thy saints have dwelt secure;
Sufficient is thine arm alone,
  And our defence is sure.

3

Before the hills in order stood,
  Or earth receiv'd her frame,
From everlasting thou art God,
  To endless years the same.

4

Thy word commands our flesh to dust,
  'Return, ye sons of men':
All nations rose from earth at first,
  And turn to earth again.

5

A thousand ages in thy sight
  Are like an evening gone;
Short as the watch that ends the night
  Before the rising sun.

6
The busy tribes of flesh and blood,
  With all their lives and cares,
Are carried downwards by thy flood,
  And lost in following years.

7
Time like an ever-rolling stream
  Bears all its sons away;
They fly forgotten as a dream
  Dies at the opening day.

8
Like flowering fields the nations stand
  Pleas'd with the morning light;
The flowers beneath the mower's hand
  Lie withering ere 'tis night.

9
Our God, our help in ages past,
  Our hope for years to come,
Be thou our guard while troubles last,
  And our eternal home.

Remorse

JUAN RAMÓN JIMÉNEZ

Time must have covered it over
with roses so
it would not be remembered.

One particular rose,
that has an unexpected magic,
on top of each lonely hour of gold
or shadows,
a place just right to hold painful memories.

So that among the divine
and joyful
climbing roses, scarlet, white,
which would leave no room for the past,
the soul would be
wound into
the body.

Dawn Outside the City Walls

JUAN RAMÓN JIMÉNEZ

You can see the face of everything, and it is white—
plaster, nightmare, adobe, anemia, cold—
turned to the east. Oh closeness to life!
Hardness of life! Like something
in the body that is animal—root, slag-ends—
with the soul still not set well there—
and mineral and vegetable!
Sun standing stiffly against man,
against the sow, the cabbages, the mud wall!
—False joy, because you are merely
in time, as they say, and not in the soul!

The entire sky taken up
by moist and steaming heaps,
a horizon of dung piles.
Sour remains, here and there,
of the night. Slices
of the green moon, half-eaten,
crystal bits from false stars,
plaster, the paper ripped off, still faintly
sky-blue. The birds
not really awake yet, in the raw moon,
streetlight nearly out.
Mob of beings and things!
—A true sadness, because you are really deep
in the soul, as they say, not in time at all!

Whoever grasps

RAINER MARIA RILKE

Whoever grasps the thousand contradictions of his life,
pulls them together into a single image, that man, joyful
and thankful, drives the rioters out of the palace,
becomes celebratory in a *different* way, and you are the guest
whom he receives on the quiet evenings.

You are the second person in his solitude,
the tranquil hub of his talking with himself;
and every circle he draws around you
lifts him out of time on those compass legs.

I have many brothers in the South

RAINER MARIA RILKE

I have many brothers in the South.
Laurels stand there in monastery gardens.
I know in what a human way they imagine the Madonna,
and I think often of young Titians
through whom God walks burning.

Yet no matter how deeply I go down into myself
my God is dark, and like a webbing made
of a hundred roots, that drink in silence.
I know that my trunk rose from his warmth, but that's all,
because my branches hardly move at all
near the ground, and just wave a little in the wind.

It is an honorable thought
EMILY DICKINSON

It is an honorable thought
And makes one lift one's hat,
As one met sudden gentlefolk
Upon a daily street,

That we've immortal place
Though pyramids decay
And kingdoms like the orchard
Flit russetly away.

Introduction

WILLIAM BLAKE

Hear the voice of the bard,
Who present, past, and future, sees;
Whose ears have heard
The Holy Word
That walked among the ancient trees;

Calling the lapsed soul,
And weeping in the evening dew;
That might control
The starry pole,
And fallen, fallen light renew!

"O Earth, O Earth, return!
Arise from out the dewy grass!
Night is worn,
And the morn
Rises from the slumbrous mass.

Turn away no more;
Why wilt thou turn away?
The starry floor,
The watery shore,
Is given thee till the break of day."

Jerusalem

WILLIAM BLAKE

And did those feet in ancient time
Walk upon England's mountains green?
And was the holy Lamb of God
On England's pleasant pastures seen?

And did the Countenance Divine
Shine forth upon our clouded hills?
And was Jerusalem builded here
Among these dark Satanic Mills?

Bring me my Bow of burning gold!
Bring me my Arrows of desire!
Bring me my Spear! O clouds, unfold!
Bring me my Chariot of fire!

I will not cease from Mental Fight,
Nor shall my Sword sleep in my hand,
Till we have built Jerusalem
In England's green and pleasant land.

The Habit of Perfection

GERARD MANLEY HOPKINS

Elected Silence, sing to me
And beat upon my whorlèd ear,
Pipe me to pastures still and be
The music that I care to hear.

Shape nothing, lips; be lovely-dumb:
It is the shut, the curfew sent
From there where all surrenders come
Which only makes you eloquent.

Be shellèd, eyes, with double dark
And find the uncreated light:
This ruck and reel which you remark
Coils, keeps, and teases simple sight.

Palate, the hutch of tasty lust,
Desire not to be rinsed with wine:
The can must be so sweet, the crust
So fresh that come in fasts divine!

Nostrils, your careless breath that spend
Upon the stir and keep of pride,
What relish shall the censers send
Along the sanctuary side!

O feel-of-primrose hands, O feet
That want the yield of plushy sward,
But you shall walk the golden street
And you unhouse and house the Lord.

And, Poverty, be thou the bride
And now the marriage feast begun,
And lily-coloured clothes provide
Your spouse not laboured-at nor spun.

The wind, one brilliant day
ANTONIO MACHADO

The wind, one brilliant day, called
to my soul with an odor of jasmine.

"In return for the odor of my jasmine,
I'd like all the odor of your roses."

"I have no roses; all the flowers
in my garden are dead."

"Well then, I'll take the withered petals
and the yellow leaves and the waters of the fountain."

The wind left. And I wept. And I said to myself:
"What have you done with the garden that was entrusted
    to you?"

Sorrow, it is not true that I know you

ANTONIO MACHADO

Sorrow, it is not true that I know you;
you are the nostalgia for a good life,
and the aloneness of the soul in shadow,
the sailing ship without wreck and without guide.

Like an abandoned dog who cannot find
a smell or a track and roams
along the roads, with no road, like
the child who in a night of the fair

gets lost among the crowd,
and the air is dusty, and the candles
fluttering,—astounded, his heart
weighed down by music and by pain;

that's how I am, drunk, sad by nature,
a mad and lunar guitarist, a poet,
and an ordinary man lost in dreams,
searching constantly for God among the mists.

The Pulley

GEORGE HERBERT

When God at first made man,
Having a glass of blessings standing by,
"Let us" (said he) "pour on him all we can;
Let the world's riches, which dispersed lie,
Contract into a span."

So strength first made a way;
Then beauty flowed, then wisdom, honour, pleasure.
When almost all was out, God made a stay,
Perceiving that alone of all his treasure
Rest in the bottom lay.

"For if I should" (said he)
"Bestow this jewel also on my creature,
He would adore my gifts instead of me,
And rest in Nature, not the God of Nature;
So both should losers be.

Yet let him keep the rest,
But keep them with repining restlessness.
Let him be rich and weary, that at least,
If goodness lead him not, yet weariness
May toss him to my breast."

from *The Hymn of Jesus*

FROM THE ACTS OF JOHN

I want to be saved . . . and I want to save. Amen.

I want to be set free . . . and I want to free. Amen.

I want to be born . . . and I want to give birth. Amen.

I want to hear . . . and I want to be heard.

Sweetness dances. I want to pipe; all of you dance. Amen.

I want to run away . . . and I want to stay. Amen.

I want to make you beautiful . . . and I want to be beautiful.
   Amen.

I want to join with you . . . and I want to be joined. Amen.

I have no house . . . and I have houses. Amen.

I have no ground . . . and I have ground. Amen.

I have no temple . . . and I have temples. Amen.

If you look at me . . . I will be a lamp. Amen.

If you see me . . . I will be a mirror. Amen.

If you knock on me . . . I will be a door. Amen.

If you are a traveller . . . I will be a road. Amen.

   This is my dance . . . Answer me with dancing.

Loss of Memory

KATHLEEN RAINE

The holy words: why did we let them go?
Whose are our children, who no longer know
"Our father who art in heaven"?
For words create that heaven, and that Father,
Hallow the holy Name,
Unspoken in a time that has forgotten
The language that peoples unseen heaven
And visible earth with all her creatures,
Tells the thousand stories of our one human story.
What but the word has made kings royal, women beautiful,
Made Mary the Mother of God? God has no mother now,
Nor Eve the far hope of her lost garden.
Disinherited from ancestral wisdom
Whose realm protected once, for us
The soundless voice of memory speaks no more
That used to tell, over and over,
The healing words: "Let not your heart be troubled,"
Of green pastures and still waters
And the twelve signs of love that never fails.

God's Grandeur

GERARD MANLEY HOPKINS

The world is charged with the grandeur of God.
  It will flame out, like shining from shook foil;
  It gathers to a greatness, like the ooze of oil
Crushed. Why do men then now not reck his rod?
Generations have trod, have trod, have trod;
  And all is seared with trade; bleared, smeared with toil;
  And wears man's smudge and shares man's smell: the soil
Is bare now, nor can foot feel, being shod.

And for all this, nature is never spent;
  There lives the dearest freshness deep down things;
And though the last lights off the black West went
  Oh, morning, at the brown brink eastward, springs—
Because the Holy Ghost over the bent
  World broods with warm breast and with ah! bright
  wings.

Pied Beauty

GERARD MANLEY HOPKINS

Glory be to God for dappled things—
   For skies of couple-colour as a brinded cow;
     For rose-moles all in stipple upon trout that swim;
Fresh-firecoal chestnut-falls; finches' wings;
   Landscape plotted and pieced—fold, fallow, and plough;
     And áll trádes, their gear and tackle and trim.

All things counter, original, spare, strange;
   Whatever is fickle, freckled (who knows how?)
     With swift, slow; sweet, sour; adazzle, dim;
He fathers-forth whose beauty is past change:
                    Praise him.

I'm ceded—I've stopped being Their's—

EMILY DICKINSON

I'm ceded—I've stopped being Their's—
The name They dropped upon my face
With water, in the country church
Is finished using, now,
And They can put it with my Dolls,
My childhood, and the string of spools,
I've finished threading—too—

Baptized, before, without the choice,
But this time, consciously, of Grace—
Unto supremest name—
Called to my Full—The Crescent dropped—
Existence's whole Arc, filled up,
With one small Diadem.

My second Rank—too small the first—
Crowned—Crowing—on my Father's breast—
A half unconscious Queen—
But this time—Adequate—Erect,
With Will to choose, or to reject,
And I choose, just a Crown—

Come to the orchard in Spring

RUMI

Come to the orchard in Spring.
There is light and wine, and sweethearts in the pomegranate
    flowers.
If you do not come, these do not matter.
If you do come, these do not matter.

Translated by Coleman Barks

III

*The Question of Greed
and Constant Hunger*

The poems at the start of this book hint at difficulty. Some force appears to challenge anyone who wants to live a spiritual life. Rumi, Donne and other poets in this third section work to make that force more visible and more vivid.

Some believe that calling this force Satan, as Western theologians sometimes do, projects it too far outward, since Satan has his kingdom elsewhere. Thinkers and poets in the Muslim world try to bring the force in closer to our lives and to our personalities. Their name for the interfering force is the Nafs.

The word Nafs simply means soul in Arabic, and it is a shortening of the phrase Al-Nafs Al-Amara—the lower or bitter soul. The word Nafs is a name then for the lower soul, and the soul that is constantly and actively engaged in wanting. It is the "wanting-creature" or the Greedy One.

The Muslims consider this eating, wanting energy to be our inheritance from those prehuman ages in which we were animals. Christianity uses the word "carnal," which points to sexuality. The Muslim world says what we have actually inherited from animals are teeth and claws. That is why Rumi refers to the Nafs sometimes as the "animal soul" or the "bodily soul." One can dream of it as a worn-out donkey; but if the human being does not work with it, it can grow to be a dragon. When it is that size, it is virtually unkillable. Rumi describes all that in his poem about the snake-catcher who one day brings home a frozen dragon which thaws out. Thousands die.

Dr. Javad Nurbakhsh, the master of the Nematullahi Sufi

order of Iran, who has written the best book in English to date on the Nafs, says that the Nafs always desires that which is prohibited. It is arrogant, it likes compliments and praise, it is more hostile than any enemy, and it may sometimes be torpid like a dragon frozen by the cold. Above all, the Nafs is greedy and hates discipline or privacy. A well-known saint who prayed each day at the front of the mosque thought he was free of the Nafs. But one day he came late and had to pray from the back of the mosque. His Nafs became furious; and the saint realized that the Nafs can simulate prayer, as long as the person praying is receiving praise. After that, he prayed in secret.*

The fondness for malls, the power of advertising in this century, and the gradual destruction of privacy in the United States, imply that the Nafs is getting its way.

---

*Dr. Javad Nurbakhsh, *The Psychology of Sufism* (New York and London: Khaniqahi-Nematullahi Publications).

Breaking the Dragon

RUMI

The animal soul has given birth to all the fetishes.
A fetish made of wood is a little like a garter snake,
But a fetish made of energy is closer to a dragon.

To snap a wooden idol in two is extremely easy;
But to break a dragon is a task beyond our power.

My friend, if you're interested in the character of the insa-
      tiable soul,
Read an account of the seven gates of Hell.

Cunning evasions flow out of the insatiable soul
In every breath we take, and in that breath-stream
A hundred Pharaohs and all their armies could drown.

GREED AND CONSTANT HUNGER

A Small Green Island

RUMI

There is a small green island
where one white cow lives alone,
a meadow of an island.

The cow grazes till nightfall, full and fat,
but during the night she panics
and grows thin as a single hair. "What shall I eat
tomorrow? There's nothing left!"

By dawn, the grass has grown up again, waist-high.
The cow starts eating and by dark
the meadow is clipped short.

She's full of strength and energy, but she panics
in the dark as before, and grows
abnormally thin overnight.

The cow does this over and over,
and this is all she does.

She never thinks, "This meadow has never failed
to grow back. Why should I be afraid
every night that it won't?"

The cow is the bodily soul.
The island field is this world where
that grows lean with fear and fat with blessing,

lean and fat. White cow,
don't make yourself miserable
with what's to come, or not to come.

Translated by Coleman Barks

The Snake-Catcher and the Frozen Snake

RUMI

Listen to this, and hear the mystery inside:
A snake-catcher went into the mountains to find a snake.

He wanted a friendly pet, and one that would amaze
audiences, but he was looking for a reptile, something
that has no knowledge of friendship.
                                        It was winter.
In the deep snow he saw a frighteningly huge dead snake.
He was afraid to touch it, but he did.
In fact, he dragged the thing into Baghdad,
hoping people would pay to see it.
                                This is how foolish
we've become! A human being is a mountain range!
Snakes are fascinated by *us!* Yet we sell ourselves
to look at a dead snake.
                        We are like beautiful satin
used to patch burlap. "Come see the dragon I killed,
and hear the adventures!" That's what he announced,
and a large crowd came,
                        but the dragon was not dead,
just dormant! He set up his show at a crossroads.
The ring of gawking rubes got thicker, everybody
on tiptoe, men and women, noble and peasant, all
packed together unconscious of their differences.
It was like the Resurrection!

He began to unwind the thick ropes and remove
the cloth coverings he'd wrapped it so well in.

Some little movement.
                    The hot Iraqi sun had woken
the terrible life. The people nearest started screaming.
Panic! The dragon tore easily and hungrily
loose, killing many instantly.
                         The snake-catcher stood there,
frozen. "What have I brought out of the mountains?" The
     snake
braced against a post and crushed the man and consumed
     him.

The snake is your animal-soul. When you bring it
into the hot air of your wanting-energy, warmed
by that and by the prospect of power and wealth,
it does massive damage.
                    Leave it in the snow mountains.
Don't expect to oppose it with quietness
and sweetness and wishing.
                    The *nafs* don't respond to those,
and they can't be killed. It takes a Moses to deal
with such a beast, to lead it back, and make it lie down
in the snow. But there was no Moses then.
Hundreds of thousands died.

Translated by Coleman Barks

Bread

RUMI

A sheikh and a disciple are walking quickly toward a town
where it's known there is very little to eat. The disciple
says nothing, but he is constantly afraid of going hungry.

The sheikh knows what the disciple thinks. How long
will you be frightened of the future
because you love food? You have closed the eye
of self-denial and forgotten who provides.

Don't worry. You'll have your walnuts and raisins and spe-
cial desserts.
Only the true favorites get hunger for their daily bread.
You're not one of those. Whoever loves the belly
is brought bowl after bowl from the kitchen.

When such a person dies, bread itself comes to the funeral
and makes a speech: "O corpse, you almost killed yourself
with worrying about food. Now you're gone and food
is still here, more than enough. Have some free bread."

Bread is more in love with you than you with it.
It sits and waits for days. It knows you have no will.
If you could fast, bread would jump into your lap
as lovers do with each other.

Be full with trusting,
not with these childish fears of famine.

Translated by Coleman Barks

The Animal Soul

RUMI

There's part of us that's like an itch.
Call it the *animal soul*, a foolishness
that when we're in it, we make
hundreds of others around us itchy.

And there is an intelligent soul
with another desire, more like sweet basil,
or the feel of a breeze.

Listen and be thankful even for scolding
that comes from the intelligent soul.
It flows out close to where you flowed out.

But that itchiness wants to put food
in our mouths that will make us sick,

feverish with the aftertaste of kissing
a donkey's rump. It's like blackening your robe
against a kettle without being anywhere
near a table of companionship.

The truth of being human is an empty table
made of soul-intelligence.

Gradually reduce what you give your animal soul,
the bread that after all overflows from sunlight.

The animal soul itself spilled out
and sprouted from the other.

Taste more often what nourishes your clear light,
and you'll have less use for the smoky oven.

You'll bury that baking equipment in the ground!

Translated by Coleman Barks

Four Questions

LALLA

Who is awake and who asleep?

What is this lake that is continually
oozing back into the earth?

What can a human being offer to God?

What do we most deeply want?

THE ANSWERS:

The mind is what sleeps.
What recognizes itself
as God is awake.

This always-disappearing lake
is made of our appetites,
these movings-about,
this talking and listening.

The only offering you can make to God
is your increasing awareness.

And the last desire is
to be God in human form.

Translated by Coleman Barks

Men and women now

LALLA

Men and women now, even the best,
can barely remember their past lives,

and as for the children, whose lives
are getting harder and harder,
what will they do?

A time is coming so deformed
and unnatural that pears and apples
will ripen with the apricots,

and a daughter and a mother
will leave the house every day
hand in hand to find new strangers
to lie down with.

Translated by Coleman Barks

Sometimes I forget completely

RUMI

Sometimes I forget completely
what companionship is.
Unconscious and insane, I spill sad
energy everywhere. My story
gets told in various ways: A romance,
a dirty joke, a war, a vacancy.

Divide up my forgetfulness to any number,
it will go around.
These dark suggestions that I follow,
are they part of some plan?
Friends, be careful. Don't come near me
out of curiosity, or sympathy.

Translated by Coleman Barks

from *Divine Meditations*
Sonnet I

JOHN DONNE

Thou hast made me; and shall thy work decay?
Repair me now, for now mine end doth haste;
I run to death, and death meets me as fast,
And all my pleasures are like yesterday.
I dare not move my dim eyes any way,
Despair behind, and death before doth cast
Such terror; and my feeble flesh doth waste
By sin in it, which it towards hell doth weigh.
Only thou art above, and when towards thee
By thy leave I can look, I rise again;
But our old subtle foe so tempteth me,
That not one hour I can myself sustain.
Thy Grace may wing me to prevent his art,
And thou like adamant draw mine iron heart.

GREED AND CONSTANT HUNGER

Raise me up, Lord

MIGUEL DE GUEVARA

Raise me up, Lord, who am fallen down,
void of love and fear and faith and awe;
I long to rise and in my place abide;
mine is the longing, mine the impediment.

I am, who am one only, cleft in twain;
I live and die, make merry and lament;
what I can do cannot by me be done;
I flee from evil and tarry in its toils.

I am so hardened in my obduracy
that spite the dread of losing me and thee
I never turn me from my wicked ways.

Between thy might and mercy I am torn;
in others every day I see amend,
in me I see fresh longing to offend thee.

Translated by Samuel Beckett

I was a stricken deer

WILLIAM COWPER

I was a stricken deer, that left the herd
Long since; with many an arrow deep infixt
My panting side was charg'd, when I withdrew
To seek a tranquil death in distant shades.
There was I found by one who had himself
Been hurt by th'archers. In his side he bore,
And in his hands and feet, the cruel scars.
With gentle force soliciting the darts,
He drew them forth, and heal'd, and bade me live.
Since then, with few associates, in remote
And silent woods I wander, far from those
My former partners of the peopled scene;
With few associates, and not wishing more.
Here much I ruminate, as much I may,
With other views of men and manners now
Than once, and others of a life to come.
I see that all are wand'rers, gone astray
Each in his own delusions; they are lost
In chase of fancied happiness, still woo'd
And never won. Dream after dream ensues;
And still they dream that they shall still succeed.
And still are disappointed. Rings the world
With the vain stir. I sum up half mankind,
And add two-thirds of the remaining half,
And find the total of their hopes and fears

Dreams, empty dreams. The million flit as gay
As if created only like the fly,
That spreads his motley wings in th' eye of noon,
To sport their season, and be seen no more.

Jesus on the lean donkey

RUMI

Jesus on the lean donkey,
this is an emblem of how the rational intellect
should control the animal-soul.

       Let your Spirit
be strong like Jesus.

      If that part becomes weak,
then the worn-out donkey grows to a dragon.

Be grateful when what seems unkind
comes from a wise person.

      Once, a holy man,
riding his donkey, saw a snake crawling into
a sleeping man's mouth! He hurried, but he couldn't
prevent it. He hit the man several blows with his club.

The man woke terrified and ran beneath an apple tree
with many rotten apples on the ground.

         "Eat!
You miserable wretch! Eat."

      "Why are you doing this to me?"
"Eat more, you fool."

      "I've never seen you before!
Who are you? Do you have some inner quarrel with my
  soul?"

The wise man kept forcing him to eat, and then he ran him.
For hours he whipped the poor man and made him run.
Finally, at nightfall, full of rotten apples,

GREED AND CONSTANT HUNGER

fatigued, bleeding, he fell
and vomited everything,
the good and the bad, the apples and the snake.

When he saw that ugly snake
come out of himself, he fell on his knees
before his assailant.
"Are you Gabriel? Are you God?
I bless the moment you first noticed me. I was dead
and didn't know it. You've given me a new life.
Everything I've said to you was stupid!
I didn't know."
"If I had explained what I was doing,
you might have panicked and died of fear.
Muhammed said,
'If I described the enemy that lives
inside men, even the most courageous would be paralyzed.
No one would go out, or do any work. No one would pray
or fast, and all power to change would fade from
human beings,'
so I kept quiet
while I was beating you, that like David
I might shape iron, so that, impossibly,
I might put feathers back into a bird's wing.

God's Silence is necessary, because of humankind's
faintheartedness. If I had told you about the snake,
you wouldn't have been able to eat, and if
you hadn't eaten, you wouldn't have vomited.

I saw your condition and drove my donkey hard
into the middle of it, saying always under my breath,
'Lord, make it easy on him.' I wasn't permitted
to tell you, and I wasn't permitted to stop
beating you!"
                    The healed man, still kneeling,
"I have no way to thank you for the quickness
of your wisdom and the strength
of your guidance.
                    God will thank you."

Translated by Coleman Barks

Who makes these changes?
RUMI

Who makes these changes?
I shoot an arrow right.
It lands left.
I ride after a deer and find myself
chased by a hog.
I plot to get what I want
and end up in prison.
I dig pits to trap others
and fall in.

I should be suspicious
of what I want.

Translated by Coleman Barks

GREED AND CONSTANT HUNGER

Difficulties

KABIR

Friend, please tell me what I can do about this mud world
I keep spinning out of myself!

I gave up expensive clothes, and bought a robe
But I noticed one day the cloth was well-woven.

So I bought some burlap, but I still
Throw it elegantly over my left shoulder.

I stopped being a sexual elephant,
And now I discover that I'm angry a lot.

I finally gave up anger, and now I notice
That I am greedy all day.

I worked hard at dissolving the greed,
And now I am proud of myself.

When the mind wants to break its link with the world
It still holds on to one thing.

Kabir says: Listen, my friend,
There are very few that find the path!

What I said to the wanting-creature

KABIR

I said to the wanting-creature inside me:
What is this river you want to cross?
There are no travelers on the river-road, and no road.
Do you see anyone moving about on that bank, or resting?
There is no river at all, and no boat, and no boatman.
There is no towrope either, and no one to pull it.
There is no ground, no sky, no time, no bank, no ford!

And there is no body, and no mind!
Do you believe there is some place that will make the soul
    less thirsty?
In that great absence you will find nothing.

Be strong then, and enter into your own body;
there you have a solid place for your feet.
Think about it carefully!
Don't go off somewhere else!

Kabir says this: just throw away all thoughts of imaginary
    things,
and stand firm in that which you are.

And where is he?

RAINER MARIA RILKE

And where is he, the clear one, whose tone rings to us?
Why don't the poor feel him, the rejoicing one,
mastering us, the young one, even though far off?

Why doesn't he climb then in their dusk—
   the great evening star of poverty.

IV

Twenty Poems of Kabir

The fourth group is made up entirely of poems from Kabir. He was born somewhere around 1398. His spiritual inheritance was both Hindu and Muslim. He was found on the streets, presumably from Hindu parents, and brought up by a Muslim couple. He is thought to have been a weaver, thought to have been married with children, thought to have lived outside both orthodox Hindu and and orthodox Muslim communities. Kabir expresses this complicated relationship by dropping suddenly from high, elevated language to the vernacular; that is one of the marks of his poetry. Yet we also know that he belonged to the disciplined, intense and exacting guru tradition of Indian spirituality. His poems, like the poems of Baul street singers, are sung to everyone; in his poems there are none of the usual distinctions between Muslims and Hindus or between men and women. And yet some poems contain theological concepts so complicated that they are clearly intended for close disciples, and no one really knows what they mean. He wants faithfulness over years. He mocks the kind of people that move from one sect to another, from Unitarianism to Buddhism to rolfing to fundamentalism:

Kabir says: Actually you are going in a hearse to the country of death,
bound hand and foot!

He belongs to the Bhakti path, the path of the lover. It is a tradition that "spiritual flatness does not control."

77

The Flute

KABIR

Friend, wake up! Why do you go on sleeping?
The night is over—do you want to lose the day the same
    way?
Other women who managed to get up early have already
    found an elephant or a jewel. . . .
So much was lost already while you slept . . .
and that was so unnecessary!

The one who loves you understood, but you did not.
You forgot to make a place in your bed next to you.
Instead you spent your life playing.
In your twenties you did not grow
because you did not know who your Lord was.
Wake up! Wake up! There's no one in your bed—
He left you during the long night.

Kabir says: The only woman awake is the woman who has
    heard the flute!

The Spinning Wheel
KABIR

The woman who is separated from her lover spins at the
   spinning wheel.

The Bagdad of the body rises with its towers and gates.
Inside it the palace of intelligence has been built.

The wheel of ecstatic love turns around in the sky,
and the spinning seat is made of the sapphires of work and
   study.

This woman weaves threads that are subtle,
and the intensity of her praise makes them fine!

Kabir says: I am that woman.
I am weaving the linen of night and day.

When my Lover comes and I feel his feet,
the gift I will have for him is tears.

The Time before Death

KABIR

Friend, hope for the Guest while you are alive.
Jump into experience while you are alive!
Think . . . and think . . . while you are alive.
What you call "salvation" belongs to the time before death.

If you don't break your ropes while you're alive,
do you think
ghosts will do it after?

The idea that the soul will join with the ecstatic
just because the body is rotten—
that is all fantasy.
What is found now is found then.
If you find nothing now,
you will simply end up with an apartment in the City of
    Death.
If you make love with the divine now, in the next life you will
    have the face of satisfied desire.

So plunge into the truth, find out who the Teacher is,
    Believe in the Great Sound!

Kabir says this: When the Guest is being searched for, it is
    the intensity of the longing for the Guest that does all
    the work.
Look at me, and you will see a slave of that intensity.

The Hearse

KABIR

The spiritual athlete often changes the color of his clothes,
and his mind remains gray and loveless.

He sits inside a shrine room all day,
so that the Guest has to go outdoors and praise the rocks.

Or he drills holes in his ears, his beard grows enormous and
    matted,
people mistake him for a goat. . . .
He goes out into wilderness areas, strangles his impulses,
and makes himself neither male nor female. . . .

He shaves his skull, puts his robe in an orange vat,
reads the Bhagavad-Gita, and becomes a terrific talker.

Kabir says: Actually you are going in a hearse to the country
    of death,
bound hand and foot!

The Caller

KABIR

I don't know what sort of a God we have been talking about.

The caller calls in a loud voice to the Holy One at dusk.
Why? Surely the Holy One is not deaf.
He hears the delicate anklets that ring on the feet of an insect
    as it walks.

Go over and over your beads, paint weird designs on your
    forehead,
wear your hair matted, long, and ostentatious,
but when deep inside you there is a loaded gun, how can you
    have God?

The Pitcher

KABIR

Student, do the simple purification.

You know that the seed is inside the horse-chestnut tree;
and inside the seed there are the blossoms of the tree, and the
chestnuts, and the shade.
So inside the human body there is the seed, and inside the
seed there is the human body again.

Fire, air, earth, water, and space—if you don't want the se-
cret one,
you can't have these either.

Thinkers, listen, tell me what you know of that is not inside
the soul?
Take a pitcher full of water and set it down on the water—
now it has water inside and water outside.
We mustn't give it a name,
lest silly people start talking again about the body and the
soul.

If you want the truth, I'll tell you the truth:
Listen to the secret sound, the real sound, which is inside
you.
The one no one talks of speaks the secret sound to himself,
and he is the one who has made it all.

The Failure

KABIR

I talk to my inner lover, and I say, why such rush?
We sense that there is some sort of spirit that loves birds and
    animals and the ants—
perhaps the same one who gave a radiance to you in your
    mother's womb.
Is it logical you would be walking around entirely orphaned
    now?
The truth is you turned away yourself,
and decided to go into the dark alone.
Now you are tangled up in others, and have forgotten what
    you once knew,
and that's why everything you do has some weird failure in
    it.

The Swan

KABIR

Swan, I'd like you to tell me your whole story!
Where you first appeared, and what dark sand you are going
toward,
and where you sleep at night, and what you are looking
for. . . .

It's morning, swan, wake up, climb in the air, follow me!
I know of a country that spiritual flatness does not control,
nor constant depression,
and those alive are not afraid to die.
There wildflowers come up through the leafy floor,
and the fragrance of "I am he" floats on the wind.
There the bee of the heart stays deep inside the flower,
and cares for no other thing.

The Cloth

KABIR

Why should I flail about with words, when love
    has made the space inside me full of light?
I know the diamond is wrapped in this cloth, so why should I
    open it all the time and look?
When the pan was empty, it flew up; now that it's full, why
    bother weighing it?

The swan has flown to the mountain lake!
Why bother with ditches and holes any more?
The Holy One lives inside you—
why open your other eyes at all?

Kabir will tell you the truth: Listen, brother!
The Guest, who makes my eyes so bright,
has made love with me.

Breath

KABIR

Are you looking for me? I am in the next seat.
My shoulder is against yours.
You will not find me in stupas, not in Indian shrine rooms,
      nor in synagogues, nor in cathedrals:
not in masses, nor kirtans, not in legs winding around your
      own neck, nor in eating nothing but vegetables.
When you really look for me, you will see me instantly—
you will find me in the tiniest house of time.
Kabir says: Student, tell me, what is God?
He is the breath inside the breath.

Music

KABIR

Have you heard the music that no fingers
enter into?
Far inside the house
entangled music—
What is the sense of leaving your house?

Suppose you scrub your ethical skin until it shines,
but inside there is no music,
then what?

Mohammed's son pores over words, and points out
        this
and that,
but if his chest is not soaked dark with love,
then what?

The Yogi comes along in his famous orange.
But if inside he is colorless, then what?

Kabir says: Every instant that the sun is risen,
        if I stand in the temple, or on a balcony,
        in the hot fields, or in a walled garden,
        my own Lord is making love with me.

The Clay Jug

KABIR

Inside this clay jug there are canyons and pine
    mountains, and the maker of canyons and pine
mountains!
All seven oceans are inside, and hundreds of millions of
    stars.
The acid that tests gold is there, and the one who judges
    jewels.
And the music from the strings no one touches, and the
    source of all water.

If you want the truth, I will tell you the truth:
Friend, listen: the God whom I love is inside.

The Swing

KABIR

Between the conscious and the unconscious, the mind has
    put up a swing:
all earth creatures, even the supernovas, sway between these
    two trees,
and it never winds down.

Angels, animals, humans, insects by the million, also the
    wheeling sun and moon;
ages go by, and it goes on.

Everything is swinging: heaven, earth, water, fire,
and the secret one slowly growing a body.
Kabir saw that for fifteen seconds, and it made him a servant
    for life.

The Unknown Flute

KABIR

I know the sound of the ecstatic flute,
  but I don't know whose flute it is.

A lamp burns and has neither wick nor oil.

A lily pad blossoms and is not attached to the bottom!

When one flower opens, ordinarily dozens open.

The moon bird's head is filled with nothing but thoughts of
    the moon,
and when the next rain will come is all that the rain bird
    thinks of.

Who is it we spend our entire life loving?

The Sound

KABIR

The flute of interior time is played whether we hear it or not,
What we mean by "love" is its sound coming in.
When love hits the farthest edge of excess, it reaches a
    wisdom.
And the fragrance of that knowledge!
It penetrates our thick bodies,
it goes through walls—
Its network of notes has a structure as if a million suns were
    arranged inside.
This tune has truth in it.
Where else have you heard a sound like this?

Why Should We Part?

KABIR

Why should we two ever want to part?

Just as the leaf of the water rhubarb lives floating on the
    water,
we live as the great one and little one.

As the owl opens his eyes all night to the moon,
we live as the great one and little one.

This love between us goes back to the first humans;
it cannot *be* annihilated.

Here is Kabir's idea: as the river gives itself into the ocean,
what is inside me moves inside you.

A Place To Sit

KABIR

Don't go outside your house to see flowers.
My friend, don't bother with that excursion.
Inside your body there are flowers.
One flower has a thousand petals.
That will do for a place to sit.
Sitting there you will have a glimpse of beauty
inside the body and out of it,
before gardens and after gardens.

Rice

KABIR

I married my Lord, and meant to live with him.
But I did not live with him, I turned away,
and all at once my twenties were gone.

The night I was married all my friends sang for me,
and the rice of pleasure and the rice of pain fell on me.

Yet when all those ceremonies were over, I left, I did not go
    home with him,
and my relatives all the way home said, "It's all right."

Kabir says: Now my love energy is actually mine.
This time I will take it with me when I go,
and outside his house I will blow the horn of triumph!

Sound of Seashells

KABIR

The darkness of night is coming along fast, and
     the shadows of love close in the body and the mind.
Open the window to the west, and disappear into the air in-
     side you.

Near your breastbone there is an open flower.
Drink the honey that is all around that flower.
Waves are coming in:
there is so much magnificence near the ocean!
Listen: Sound of big seashells! Sound of bells!

Kabir says: Friend, listen, this is what I have to say:
The Guest I love is inside me!

The Boat

KABIR

The Guest is inside you, and also inside me;
you know the sprout is hidden inside the seed.
We are all struggling; none of us has gone far.
Let your arrogance go, and look around inside.

The blue sky opens out farther and farther,
the daily sense of failure goes away,
the damage I have done to myself fades,
a million suns come forward with light,
when I sit firmly in that world.

I hear bells ringing that no one has shaken;
inside "love" there is more joy than we know of;
rain pours down, although the sky is clear of clouds;
there are whole rivers of light.
The universe is shot through in all parts by a single sort of
   love.
How hard it is to feel that joy in all our four bodies!

Those who hope to be reasonable about it fail.
The arrogance of reason has separated us from that love.
With the word "reason" you already feel miles away.

How lucky Kabir is, that surrounded by all this joy
he sings inside his own little boat.
His poems amount to one soul meeting another.
These songs are about forgetting dying and loss.
They rise above both coming in and going out.

V

God in the Feminine

Christians in the West, even those with very good heart, have found difficulty in returning to the idea of the feminine in God, or the idea of God in the feminine, or the idea of a God who is feminine, or even the idea that there is a God who is both masculine and feminine. Joseph Campbell used to sidestep this question entirely by saying that such language is human, all too human, and God may be like a ball of fire four feet across that passes through a room and would immediately kill anyone near. When we refer to God, we mean a being beyond categories, beyond conditions, beyond limitations, beyond opposites, and so by definition beyond gender. Such thoughts are difficult to think, and so we choose an image of a father or a mother because we are, in part, children.

That said, we have to notice that in the ancient world, philosophers and religious people, no matter how sophisticated, were perfectly willing to imagine divinities who were basically feminine in tone or masculine in tone. The ancient Greeks accepted six divinities as masculine, among them Apollo and Zeus, and six divinities as feminine, among them Aphrodite and Artemis. Dionysus, as we know, had both male and female elements.

Biblical scholars, particularly women, have begun to bring Sophia forth out of her eclipse. The translators of the Old Testament obscured her femininity by translating her name as Wisdom. For centuries Sophia had been imagined as a female being; she carried not only wisdom but discrimination and playfulness. She typically calls to people in the Mediterranean cities from the rooftops: "All you who want knowledge, come to me." The split between the Eastern Church and the Western Church turned on the rejection or acceptance of Sophia.

It's clear that the early church knew about Sophia. Paul mentions her in several letters and uses the phrase "Sophia in Christ." Susan Cady, Marian Ronan and Hel Taussig, in their book *Sophia*, say:

> One of Sophia's traits which Paul transfers directly to Jesus is Sophia's hidden, that is, yet-to-be-discovered, presence in all things which results from her participation in their coming into being. Paul acknowledges this trait of Sophia in 1 Corinthians 2:7: "The hidden Sophia of God which we teach in our mysteries is the Sophia that God predestined to be for our glory before the ages began" . . .

Such a description of Sophia is reminiscent of Wisdom 7:22, 23:

> For within her is a spirit intelligent, holy, . . . unsullied, lucid, invulnerable, benevolent, sharp, irresistible, beneficent, loving to people . . . pure and most subtle . . . she is so pure, she pervades and permeates all things.

With words such as these, we are coming close to the ancient view of the Divine Feminine as that which was always present in Creation: "She who knows your works, she who was present when the world was made."

This group of poems opens with the great prayer to nature which comes not from the Hebraic traditions but from the archaic Greek traditions. Religious knowledge in ancient

Greece was carried in two streams. The more public, Homeric stream is the one we know best; but the deeper, more secret tradition, of which little has survived in written form, is called the Orphic stream. The hymn that follows comes from the Orphic liturgy.

To Nature

I call to Nature, the mother of all, the mother who makes,
Heavenly, honored, goddess of wealth, sovereign,
The one who wins, who is never tamed, the narrator, the
    Giver of light,
Stronger than the strongest, who gives her breasts to all,
Who never dies, the firstborn, known in legends, who helps
    us do,
Born of the night, all wisdom, carrier of light, a strong
    holder-back,
We see your footprints that whirl silently when you are still,
O holy one, heavenly mother of all Gods,
Who never dies, who brings all round, belonging to all, but
    yours only,
Father of yourself, but without father, much loved, sunny,
    immense,
Rose-like, with braids of flowers, adored, open to us, wise,
Forerunner, she who gets things done, giver of breath, feeder
    of all, virgin,
Enough-in-herself, just, with all three Graces inside,
    commanding
Goddess of earth, sea, and air,
Bitter to the picayune, sweet to the large-hearted,
Wholly wise, wholly generous, guardian Queen,
Provider of food, pouring ripening grain over our heads,

You are father, you are mother, you are nurturer, you are
    nurse,
Giver of a swift birth, throned, seed-rich, ancestor of sea-
    sons,
Creator of the world, sculptor, spring of richness, diversity
    of the sea,
Everlasting one, she who gets things to move, wholly wise,
    one who cares,
And never fails, one whose strong energy goes whirling,
Always river-like, moving in circles, changer of shores,
Receiving honor on your elegant throne, solitary, you finish
    your design,
Among deep thunder sounds you sit above Kings and
    Queens,
Having no fear, champion over all, you are fate, and des-
    tiny's fiery Mother,
Never born or dying, you are continuous life and know what
    comes.
You are the Great Plenum and you alone give birth.
Holy Mother, we pray you in this season lead us
On to peace and health and increase of good things.

You are the future

RAINER MARIA RILKE

You are the future, the immense morning sky
turning red over the prairies of eternity.
You are the rooster-crow after the night of time,
the dew, the early devotions, and the Daughter,
the Guest, the Ancient Mother, and Death.

You are the shape that changes its own shape,
that climbs out of fate, towering,
that which is never shouted for, and never mourned for,
and no more explored than a savage wood.

You are the meaning deepest inside things,
that never reveals the secret of its owner.
And how you look depends on where we are:
from a boat you are shore, from the shore a boat.

GOD IN THE FEMININE

Prayer to the Mother
APULEIUS, *THE GOLDEN ASS*
LUCIUS'S PRAYER TO BE CHANGED AGAIN
FROM A DONKEY TO A MAN

"Blessed Queen of Heaven, whether you are pleased to be
known as Ceres, the original harvest mother who in joy at
the finding of your lost daughter Proserpine abolished the
rude acorn diet of our forefathers and gave them bread raised
from the fertile soil of Eleusis; or whether as celestial Venus,
now adored at sea-girt Paphos, who at the time of the first
Creation coupled the sexes in mutual love and so contrived
that man should continue to propagate his kind for ever; or
whether as Artemis, the physician sister of Phoebus Apollo,
reliever of the birth pangs of women, and now adored in the
ancient shrine at Ephesus; or whether as dread Proserpine to
whom the owl cries at night, whose triple face is potent
against the malice of ghosts, keeping them imprisoned below
earth; you who wander through many sacred groves and are
propitiated with many different rites—you whose womanly
light illumines the walls of every city, whose misty radiance
nurses the happy seeds under the soil, you who control the
wandering course of the sun and the very power of his
rays—I beseech you, by whatever name, in whatever aspect,
with whatever ceremonies you deign to be invoked, have
mercy on me in my extreme distress, restore my shattered
fortune, grant me repose and peace after this long sequence
of miseries. End my sufferings and perils, rid me of this hate-
ful four-footed disguise, return me to my family, make me
Lucius once more."

Translated by Robert Graves

PART V

White Buffalo Woman

JOHN G. NEIHARDT, *BLACK ELK SPEAKS*

There is a story about the way the pipe first came to us. A very long time ago, they say, two scouts were out looking for bison; and when they came to the top of a high hill and looked north, they saw something coming a long way off, and when it came closer they cried out, "It is a woman!," and it was. Then one of the scouts, being foolish, had bad thoughts and spoke them; but the other said: "That is a sacred woman; throw all bad thoughts away." When she came still closer, they saw that she wore a fine white buckskin dress, that her hair was very long and that she was very young and very beautiful. And she knew their thoughts and said in a voice that was like singing: "You do not know me, but if you want to do as you think, you may come." And the foolish one went; but just as he stood before her, there was a white cloud that came and covered them. And the beautiful young woman came out of the cloud, and when it blew away the foolish man was a skeleton covered with worms.

Then the woman spoke to the one who was not foolish: "You shall go home and tell your people that I am coming and that a big tepee shall be built for me in the center of the nation." And the man, who was very much afraid, went quickly and told the people, who did at once as they were told; and there around the big tepee they waited for the sacred woman. And after a while she came, very beautiful and singing, and as she went into the tepee this is what she sang:

"With visible breath I am walking.
A voice I am sending as I walk.

GOD IN THE FEMININE

In a sacred manner I am walking.
With visible tracks I am walking.
In a sacred manner I walk."

And as she sang, there came from her mouth a white cloud that was good to smell. Then she gave something to the chief, and it was a pipe with a bison calf carved on one side to mean the earth that bears and feeds us, and with twelve eagle feathers hanging from the stem to mean the sky and the twelve moons, and these were tied with a grass that never breaks, "Behold!" she said. "With this you shall multiply and be a good nation. Nothing but good shall come from it. Only the hands of the good shall take care of it and the bad shall not even see it." Then she sang again and went out of the tepee; and as the people watched her going, suddenly it was a white bison galloping away and snorting, and soon it was gone.

This they tell, and whether it happened so or not I do not know; but if you think about it, you can see that it is true.

I sing of a maiden

ANONYMOUS

I sing of a maiden
 That is makèless:
King of all kingès
 To her son she ches.

He came all so stillè
 There his mother was,
As dew in Aprillè
 That falleth on the grass.

He came all so stillè
 To his mother's bower,
As dew in Aprillè
 That falleth on the flower.

He came all so stillè
 There his mother lay,
As dew in Aprillè
 That falleth on the spray.

Mother and maiden
 Was never none but she;
Well may such a lady
 Goddès mother be.

For the flowers are great blessings
CHRISTOPHER SMART

For the flowers are great blessings,
For the Lord made a Nosegay in the meadow with his disci-
ples and preached upon the lily.
For the angels of God took it out of his hand and carried it
to the Height . . .
For there is no Height in which there are not flowers.
For flowers have great virtues for all the senses.
For the flower glorifies God and the root parries the adver-
sary.
For the flowers have their angels even the words of God's
Creation.
For the warp and woof of flowers are worked by perpetual
moving spirits.
For flowers are good both for the living and the dead.
For there is a language of flowers.
For there is a sound reasoning upon all flowers.
For elegant phrases are nothing but flowers.
For flowers are peculiarly the poetry of Christ.
For flowers are medicinal.
For flowers are musical in ocular harmony.
For the right names of flowers are yet in heaven, God make
gardeners better nomenclators.
For the Poorman's nosegay is an introduction to a
Prince . . .

To Aphrodite of the Flowers, at Knossos

SAPPHO

Leave Crete and come to this holy temple
where the pleasant grove of apple trees
circles an altar smoking with frank-
    incense.

Here roses leave shadow on the ground
and cold springs babble through apple branches
where shuddering leaves pour down pro-
    found sleep.

In our meadow where horses graze
and wild flowers of spring blossom,
anise shoots fill the air with a-
    roma.

And here, Queen Aphrodite, pour
heavenly nectar into gold cups
and fill them gracefully with sud-
    den joy.

Translated by Willis Barnstone

GOD IN THE FEMININE

Lord, help me

FRENCH MEDIEVAL PRAYER

Lord, help me . . .
Because my boat is so small,
And your sea is so immense.

from *Random Thoughts on the Love of God*

SIMONE WEIL

. . . Creatures speak in sounds. The word of God is silence. The secret word of God's love can be nothing but silence. Christ is the silence of God. There is no tree like the cross. No harmony like the silence of God. The Pythagoreans knew this harmony in the endless silence that surrounds the stars. Necessity, here below, is the resonance of God's silence.

Our soul makes constant noise, but it has a silent place we never hear. When the silence of God enters us, pierces our soul and joins its silent secret place, then God is our treasure and our heart. And space opens before us like a fruit that breaks in two. Then we see the universe from a point beyond space.

Translated by Carol Cosman

PART V

The Red Goddess (Laksmi)
FROM *HYMN TO TIRUMAL*

Wearing jewels
many-colored as rainbows
   bent across the high heavens
on your chest, itself a jewel
studded with pendant pearls,
you always wear the Red Goddess
as the moon wears
his shadow.

        Which doesn't agree at all
with those who read the Vedas
and say,

        You as the Boar,
with white tusks, sharp and spotted,
washed by the rising waves,
you lifted up and married
the Earth-maiden,

so not a spot of earth
is ever troubled by the sea.

Translated by A. K. Ramanujan

GOD IN THE FEMININE

There is a lake

LALLA

There is a lake so tiny
that a mustard seed would cover it
easily, yet everyone drinks from this lake.

Deer, jackals, rhinoceroses, and sea elephants
keep falling into it, falling and dissolving
almost before they have time to be born.

Translated by Coleman Barks

Your way of knowing

LALLA

Your way of knowing is a private herb garden.
Enclose it with a hedge of meditation,
and self-discipline, and helpfulness to others.

Then everything you've done before
will be brought as a sacrifice
to the mother goddess.

And each day, as you eat the herbs,
the garden grows more bare and empty.

Translated by Coleman Barks

You were once a swan

LALLA

You were once a swan singing
melodies, Lalla. Now you're quiet.

Someone, I don't know who, has run off
with what belonged to you.

The millstone stops, and the hole
where the grain is fed in fills

with grain. The channel leading
to the grinding work is covered over

and hidden, and the miller
himself has disappeared.

Translated by Coleman Barks

The Goddess

THÉODORE DE BANVILLE

She had opened an immense hole in the soft ground, which she quickly digs up with her skeleton fingers, and bending her ribs and inclining her white smooth skull, she heaps together in the abyss old men and youths, women and children, cold, pale, and stiff, whose lids she silently closes.

"Ah," sighs the dreamer, who sadly and with heavy heart sees her accomplish her work, "accursed, accursed be thou, destroyer of beings, detestable and cruel Death, and mayest thou be dominated and desolated by the ever-renewed floods of mortal life!"

The grave-digger has arisen. She turns her face; she is now made of pink and charming flesh; her friendly brow is crowned with rosy corals. She bears in her arms fair naked children, who laugh to the sky, and she says softly to the dreamer, while gazing at him with eyes full of joy:

"I am she who accomplishes without cease and without end the transformation of all. Beneath my fingers the flowers that have become cinders bloom once more, and I am both She whom thou namest Death, and She whom thou namest Life!"

Translated by Stuart Merrill

To Juan at the Winter Solstice

ROBERT GRAVES

There is one story and one story only
That will prove worth your telling,
Whether as learned bard or gifted child;
To it all lines or lesser gauds belong
That startle with their shining
Such common stories as they stray into.

Is it of trees you tell, their months and virtues,
Of strange beasts that beset you,
Of birds that croak at you the Triple will?
Or of the Zodiac and how slow it turns
Below the Boreal Crown,
Prison of all true kings that ever reigned?

Water to water, ark again to ark,
From woman back to woman:
So each new victim treads unfalteringly
The never altered circuit of his fate,
Bringing twelve peers as witness
Both to his starry rise and starry fall.

Or is it of the Virgin's silver beauty,
All fish below the thighs?
She in her left hand bears a leafy quince;
When with her right hand she crooks a finger, smiling,
How may the King hold back?
Royally then he barters life for love.

GOD IN THE FEMININE

Or of the undying snake from chaos hatched,
Whose coils contain the ocean,
Into whose chops with naked sword he springs,
Then in black water, tangled by the reeds,
Battles three days and nights,
To be spewed up beside her scalloped shore?

Much snow is falling, winds roar hollowly,
The owl hoots from the elder,
Fear in your heart cries to the loving-cup:
Sorrow to sorrow as the sparks fly upward.
The log groans and confesses
There is one story and one story only.

Dwell on her graciousness, dwell on her smiling,
Do not forget what flowers
The great boar trampled down in ivy time.
Her brow was creamy as the long ninth wave,
Her sea-blue eyes were wild.
But nothing promised that is not performed.

Love's Maturity

HADEWIJCH OF ANTWERP

In the beginning Love satisfies us.
When Love first spoke to me of love—
How I laughed at her in return!
But then she made me like the hazel trees,
Which blossom early in the season of darkness,
And bear fruit slowly.

Translated by Oliver Davies

Knowing Love in Herself

HADEWIJCH OF ANTWERP

I do not complain of suffering for Love,
It is right that I should always obey her,
For I can know her only as she is in herself,
Whether she commands in storm or in stillness.
This is a marvel beyond my understanding,
Which fills my whole heart
And makes me stray in a wild desert.

Translated by Oliver Davies

Briefly It Enters, and Briefly Speaks

JANE KENYON

I am the blossom pressed in a book,
found again after two hundred years. . . .

I am the maker, the lover, and the keeper. . . .

When the young girl who starves
sits down to a table
she will sit beside me. . . .

I am food on the prisoner's plate. . . .

I am water rushing to the well-head,
filling the pitcher until it spills. . . .

I am the patient gardener
of the dry and weedy garden. . . .

I am the stone step,
the latch, and the working hinge. . . .

I am the heart contracted by joy . . .
the longest hair, white
before the rest. . . .

I am there in the basket of fruit
presented to the widow. . . .

I am the musk rose opening
unattended, the fern on the boggy summit. . . .

I am the one whose love
overcomes you, already with you
when you think to call my name. . . .

Sonnet XII

EDNA ST. VINCENT MILLAY

Olympian gods, mark now my bedside lamp
Blown out; and be advised too late that he
Whom you call sire is stolen into the camp
Of warring Earth, and lies abed with me.
Call out your golden hordes, the harm is done:
Enraptured in his great embrace I lie;
Shake heaven with spears, but I shall bear a son
Branded with godhead, heel and brow and thigh.
Whom think not to bedazzle or confound
With meteoric splendours or display
Of blackened moons or suns or the big sound
Of sudden thunder on a silent day;
Pain and compassion shall he know, being mine,—
Confusion never, that is half divine.

GOD IN THE FEMININE

The Mysteries Remain
H.D.

The mysteries remain,
I keep the same
cycle of seed-time
and of sun and rain;
Demeter in the grass,
I multiply,
renew and bless
Iacchus in the vine;
I hold the law,
I keep the mysteries true,
the first of these
to name the living, dead;
I am red wine and bread.

I keep the law,
I hold the mysteries true,
I am the vine,
the branches, you
and you.

A Flower No More than Itself

LINDA GREGG

She was there on the mountain,
still as the fig tree and the failed wheat.
Only the lizards and a few goats moved.
Everything stunned by heat and silence.
I would get to the top of the terraced starkness
with my ankles cut by thistles and all of me
drained by the effort in the fierce light.
I would put the pomegranate and the anise
and a few daisies on the great rock
where the fountain was long ago.
Too tired to praise. And found each time
tenderness and abundance in the bareness.
Went back down knowing I would sleep clean.
That She would be awake all year with sun
and dirt and rain. Pride Her life.
All nature Her wealth. Sound of owls Her pillow.

There is no one

EDITH SÖDERGRAN

There is no one in this world who has time
but God alone.
And therefore all flowers come to Him
and the least among the ants.

The forget-me-not asks Him for a stronger brilliance
in her blue eyes
and the ant asks Him for more strength
to grip the straw.
And the bees ask Him for a stronger victory song
among scarlet roses.

And God is present in everything.
When the old woman unexpectedly met her cat at the well
and the cat his mistress
the joy was great for both of them
but greater still was their knowledge that God had brought
     them together
and wished them this wonderful friendship
for fourteen years.

Meanwhile, a redstart flew out of the mountain ash by the
     well
happy that God had not allowed the hunter to catch him.
But in a vague dream a little worm saw
how the crescent moon split his being into two:
one was nothing,
the other one was everything and God Himself.

Translated by Stina Katchadourian

Lay your head

LAKSHMINKARA

Lay your head on a block of butter and chop—
Break the blade of the axe!
The woodcutter laughs!
A frog swallows an elephant!

It's amazing, Mekhala,
Do not doubt.
If it confounds you, o seeker,
Drop concepts now!

My teacher didn't tell me,
I didn't understand—
Flowers blossomed in the sky!

It's marvelous, Mekhala,
Have no doubt!
If you're incredulous, adept,
Drop your doubts!

A barren woman gives birth!
A chair dances!
Because cotton is expensive,
The naked weep!

. . . .

Amazing! An elephant sits on a throne
Held up by two bees!

125

Incredible! The sightless lead,
The mute speak!

.   .   .   .

Amazing! A mouse chases a cat!
An elephant flees from a crazy donkey!

It's marvelous, Mekhala,
Do not doubt!
If you're stunned, adept,
Drop your doubts!

Amazing! A hungry monkey eats rocks!
Wonderful—the experience of the mind!
Who can express it?

Translated by Miranda Shaw

How shall I begin my song?

OWL WOMAN

How shall I begin my song
In the blue night that is settling?

In the great night my heart will go out,
Toward me the darkness comes rattling.
In the great night my heart will go out.

Brown owls come here in the blue evening,
They are hooting about,
They are shaking their wings and hooting.

Black Butte is far.
Below it I had my dawn.
I could see the daylight
coming back for me.

The morning star is up.
I cross the mountains
into the light of the sea.

Translated by Frances Densmore

In Praise of Sophia

FROM PROVERBS: 3:11–20

Friend, don't be angry at the Teacher's discipline,
nor lose your taste for his rebukes,
for the Teacher only corrects those whom he loves,
as a mother watches constantly her favorite son.
The man who finds the ecstatic mother is a joyful man,
and the man who gains consciousness from her,
for the gain from her is better than gain from silver,
and the profit from that acquisition better than gold.
She is more precious than jewels,
and nothing you desire can compare with her.
She has long life in her right hand,
and riches and reputation in her left.
Along her path there is much pleasure,
and her path goes through the places of peace.
She is a tree of life for those who bring her inside,
those who hold her firmly inside are called happy.
The Secret One through the ecstatic mother founded the
    earth,
through consciousness he made the skies go around,
by secret knowledge the oceans broke open,
and the clouds let the dew down.

Translated by Aaron Blon

A Herd of Does

HUGH MACDIARMID

Gildermorie

There is no doe in all the herd
Whose heart is not her heart,
O Earth, with all their glimmering eyes
She sees thee as thou art.

Like them in shapes of fleeting fire
She mingles with the light
Till whoso saw her sees her not
And doubts his former sight.

They come and go and none can say
Who sees them subtly run
If they indeed are forms of life
Or figments of the sun.

So is she one with Heaven here,
Confounding mortal eyes,
As do the holy dead who move
Innumerous in the skies.

But now and then a wandering man
May glimpse as on he goes
A golden movement of her dreams
as 'twere a herd of does.

GOD IN THE FEMININE

VI

Loving God through
Loving a Woman or a Man

One of the greatest periods in Western literature occurred during the twelfth century, particularly in southern France, when the Provençal language became a medium for ecstatic poetry. The poets, both men and women, spoke of love relationships and divine relationships in the same poem. This was the time when an increased respect for women and for the feminine soul, associated historically with the concept of chivalry, was changing the consciousness of many rough people at the edges of the Islamic Empire. Recent research has indicated that the powerful concept of the chivalrous life and the orders of chivalry originated in Persian culture.

When the Albigensian religion moved into southern France, the Catholic Church called it a heresy, and sometimes referred to it as the Bogomil heresy. Religiously it shared many themes with primitive Christianity, with the old Manichaean thought and with Gnosticism, and it had clear connections with Persian and Arab culture. The emphasis was on ecstatic love. The word used for love was *amor*. It didn't escape contemporary notice that *amor* is *roma* spelled backwards. Roman Catholic priests supported the view that continuous love is possible only inside marriage, and the Albigensian enthusiasts supported the view that continuous love is possible only outside marriage.

A man living amor might, then, choose a married woman, perhaps one married to a count or lord, tell her that he was her admirer and lover, and then love her "from far away." Sometimes this love might go on twenty years with no sexual union; and other times, as Guillaume IX makes clear in his poem, there was sexual joy as well. The Countess of Die, one of the finest Provençal poets, chose a man to admire and love. With her husband she was practical; with the lover she was intense, devoted and dedicated to a spiritual quality which she could feel in the other's soul.

Denis de Rougemont describes some of this in his book called *Love in the Western World*. He takes the Catholic position and is opposed to passion on principle; but he describes the circumstances and the Arabic sources of the ecstatic practice well. By looking at some Persian poetry of this era and some Sufi poets such as Rumi and Hafez, it becomes clear that one possible interpretation of these amazing long-term relationships was that a man loved and admired a woman, but he also looked through her to the Divine Feminine on the other side. Jaufre Rudel, in his famous poem, repeats the phrase "love from far away" many times, with slightly different meanings each time. At one point he even mentions that he is aware of the Muslim origin of this practice. He says:

> she is so strong and fine, I'll tell you
> what I wish: I wish I were a prisoner
> for her in the kingdom of the Arabs!

The Countess of Die loves and admires the man she has chosen, but one could say that she also looks through the man to a Divine Masculine standing on the other side. Which figure becomes more important, the human being or the Divine glimpsed beyond, is the choice of each poet. There are no rules. What is understood is that the relationship is not to be chosen lightly, because one must be faithful for many years. Rumi says, in Coleman Barks's translation:

> I would love to kiss you.
> *The price of kissing is your life.*
>
> Now my loving is running toward my life shouting,
> *What a bargain, let's buy it.*

The Visit of the Beloved
IBN HAZM

When you came to me, it was a little before
    the Christians rang their bells,
when the half moon was climbing up the sky.

It was like the raised eyebrow of an old man,
    each hair of it white,
or like the delicate arch of your white foot.

The dawn had still not risen, yet the great
    bow of the Lord
shone against the horizon at your coming,
    radiant with every color
    like the peacock's tail.

Separation by Death
IBN HAZM

She was pure and white, resembling the sun as it rises.
All other women were merely stars!
Love for her has made my heart fly off its permanent branch,
And after stopping a while, it is still hovering in the air!

Adapted from the translation by A. R. Nykl

Chastity

IBN FARAJ

Although she was ready to give
herself to me, I abstained
and did not accept
the temptation Satan offered.

She came unveiled in the night.
Illuminated by her face,
night put aside its shadowy
veils as well.

Each one of her glances
could cause hearts to turn over.

But I clung to the divine precept
that condemns lust and reined in
the capricious horses of my passion
so that my instinct
would not rebel against chastity.

And so I passed the night with her
like a thirsty little camel
whose muzzle keeps it from nursing.

She was a field of fruit and flowers
offering one like me no other enjoyment
than sight and scent.

Know then that I am not
one of those beasts gone wild
who take gardens for pastures.

Translated by Lysander Kemp

Two Poems by Rumi

RUMI

When I am with you, we stay up all night.
When you're not here, I can't go to sleep.

Praise God for these two insomnias!
And the difference between them.

I would love to kiss you.
The price of kissing is your life.

Now my loving is running toward my life shouting,
What a bargain, let's buy it.

Translated by Coleman Barks

LOVING A WOMAN OR A MAN

In the great sweetness of the spring
GUILLAUME IX OF POITIERS

In the great sweetness of the spring,
woods turn green, and the birds
sing on, each in his own Latin,
in the new way we all know.
Then it's right that each man
come close to what he desires most.

But no messenger arrives, no letter
from the place of goodness and sweetness,
and so my body does not sleep,
it does not laugh, and I hold myself in
until I know where we are,
if this will go as I wish it to go.

Our love moves in this way:
like a branch of the hawthorn tree
that holds to its trunk, and trembles
in the rain all night, in the cold,
until morning, when the sun expands
all through the green leaves and the branches.

It reminds me of that other morning:
our sweet war we brought to an end,
and she gave me a gift so great:
her faithful valley and her ring.
I want my God to let me live
to have my hands beneath her cloak again.

I am not fond of all this Latin
that parts me from my Lovely Friend;
for I agree with that saying:
"The briefest sermon never ends."
Some people treat love with words,
but we have the bread and we have the knife.

A Certain Knight

THE COUNTESS OF DIE

For a while now a certain knight
has caused me great distress,
and I want it known, once and for all,
how excessively I have loved him;
  yet I've been betrayed
on pretext of not giving him my love,
and ever since, in bed or dressed,
  my life's been one of grief.

How I would like to hold him
one night in my naked arms
and see him joyfully use my body
as a pillow, for I am more
  in love with him
than Flore with Blanchefleur,
and offer him my heart, my love,
  my mind, my eyes and my life.

My handsome friend, gracious and charming,
when will I hold you in my power?
Oh that I might lie with you
one night and kiss you lovingly!
  Know how great is my desire
to treat you as a husband;
but you must promise me to do
  whatever I may wish.

Translated by Anthony Bonner

When the Days Grow Long in May

JAUFRE RUDEL

In the month of May when all leaves open
calls of birds from far away are sweet to me;
and then when I live parted from the singing of birds,
a love from far away fills me with grief;
I walk on, sad, bent, thoughtful in longing;
so that lilac blossoms and birds please me no more
than ice, or winter's storms, and wind, and cold.

Whoever brings me to this love
from far away, I will consider my lord—
yet, though I've received one good thing,
I get two bad; this love is far away;
ah God! I want to be a pilgrim, walking,
then I would see my stick and my cloak
a second time in her gorgeous eyes!

My joy will come when I ask her help
for the love of God, the far-off love:
and, if it pleases her, I will live
close to her, though I am far away now.
And what conversations we will have
when the far-off lover is so close
I will know the comfort of her soft words.

I will rejoice and be sad when we part then,
after I have seen my love from far away;
but when I will see her I have no idea,
because our lands are very far away:
there are so many roads, so many paths,

LOVING A WOMAN OR A MAN

and as for me, I am not a saint or prophet—
but it will all go as it pleases God!

I have no pleasure at all in love
if it is not the pleasure of the love from far away;
for I know no love gentler nor love better
anywhere, neither close by, nor far away:
she is so strong and fine, I'll tell you
what I wish: I wish I were a prisoner
for her in the kingdom of the Arabs!

God, who made everything that comes and goes,
and created this love from far away,
give me the power—the heart-strength I have—
to see this love from far away
face to face, in such a pleasant way
that the poor room and the little garden
will be to me all the time a palace!

He says the truth who says that I am craving
and full of desire for this love of far away,
because no other joy pleases me so much
as the rich joy of this love from far away.
But the way to this love is blocked:
my godfather arranged a fate for me:
I love, but no one makes love to me.

But the way to this love is blocked.
Total be the curse on my godfather, who made it
so I love, but no one makes love to me.

The woman I adore

DANTE ALIGHIERI

The woman I adore carries ecstatic love in her eyes.
Whatever she looks at grows less worldly.
When she walks past, each man turns to look at her;
And if she notices him, his chest trembles.

And then, his eyes on the ground, he turns pale;
He can feel his inadequacies inside his heart.
Self-absorption and self-mothering leave ahead of her;
All you women, help me to say this rightly.

When a man hears her voice, sweetness and thoughts
Of ways to serve others come into his body.
I say then, much praise to the first man who glimpsed her.

And when she smiles, for even a short time, there is a feeling
Of someone I cannot speak of, nor keep in remembrance.
This is all some sort of miracle, fresh, amazing.

Amor and the courteous heart
DANTE ALIGHIERI

Amor and the courteous heart are the same thing,
Just as the wise man has set down in his poems;
When one is there, the other has to be.
You know that from reason and the rational soul.

One day when She was amorous, Nature created them,
Amor as Lord and the heart as his great house,
Within that house, the Lord lies there sleeping;
Perhaps he sleeps briefly, perhaps for years.

True beauty shows itself then in a fine woman.
Her beauty so delights the eyes, that the heart
Conceives at last a desire for this sweet thing.

And sometimes Desire bustles about in the house
So long that Amor wakes from his sleep.
A woman knows this same joy with a worthy man.

The Meeting Missed

RABINDRANATH TAGORE, *GITANJALI*

If I am not to meet you again in this life then I want to feel that I have missed the meeting, don't let me forget, let me feel the pain of it in my dreams and while awake.

As the time passes in the black dust of the body, and I get fat with money, I want to feel that I have gotten nothing out of it all—don't let me forget, I want to feel the slivers of pain in my dreams and while awake.

When I walk up the steps, exhausted and tense after a long trip, or when I climb into some lonely bed, I want to feel that the long trip is still ahead of me—don't let me forget, I want to feel the pain in my legs both while asleep and while awake.

When my house is all cleaned, and drinks are set here and there, and I hear people laughing, I want to feel that I haven't invited you to my house—don't let me forget, I want to feel the pain of that grief both while asleep and while awake.

For the Goddess of Love

RABINDRANATH TAGORE, *GITANJALI*

There is a ruined temple near here. . . . No one sings now for the Holy One who was once praised there. The air is motionless and heavy above the altar.

The odor of flowers no longer pulled for you floats in through the door.

One of your old worshippers goes out every day into the cities, hoping to receive the good things that he used to ask for from you. And every day at dusk he returns five thousand miles to his temple, his shoelaces untied, his face tired.

How many good days go by! How many nights useful for worship go by, and not one candle is lit or one poem sung!

How many sculptors work the whole day with large shoulders and hair whitened with stone dust making a statue of you, and then as dusk comes carry it to the river and throw it in.

She is still in the temple, but no one gives Her food or takes food from Her, in this ignorance that never ends.

Dusk

RABINDRANATH TAGORE, *GITANJALI*

Dusk is here. Darkness starts to come up from the bushes
and the shrubs. I am going to take a walk down to the river.
How marvellous the sound of running water in the near
dark! I heard it a quarter mile away . . . at the river, solitude,
no one around, no one has come to fish, there is some wind,
small waves gallop on the light plain.

I don't know if I'll go back home tonight or not. I have the
feeling I'm going to meet someone. And sure enough, where
the footpath crosses the river, there is a boat. Floating in the
boat is a person whom I've never seen, playing a flute.

The Message

RABINDRANATH TAGORE, *GITANJALI*

I see a light, but no fire. Is this what my life is to be like? Better to head for the grave.

A messenger comes, the grief-courier, and the message is that the woman you love is in her house alone, and wants you to come now while it is still night.

Clouds unbroken, rain, all night, all night. I don't understand these wild impulses—what is happening to me.

A lightning flash is followed by deeper melancholy. I stumble around inside looking for the path the night wants me to take.

Light, where is the light? Light the fire, if you have desire! Thunder, rushing wind, nothingness. Black night, black stone. Don't let your whole life go by in the dark.

Evidently the only way to find the path is to set fire to my own life.

VII

Twenty Poems of Rumi

Rumi, the Persian poet, who was born in 1207 and died in 1273, has, to the recent amazement of many people in the Western culture as well as the Islamic culture, been able to speak directly to contemporary readers. One of the greatest pieces of good luck that has happened recently in American poetry is Coleman Barks's agreement to translate poem after poem of Rumi. Rumi, like Kabir, is able to contain and continue intricate theological arguments and at the same time speak directly from the heart or to the heart. Coleman's exquisite sensitivity to the flavor and turns of ordinary American speech has produced marvelous lines, full of flavor and Sufi humor, as well as the intimacy that is carried inside American speech at its best. He is able to follow Rumi's playfulness:

> you go on the street, the street
> where everyone says, "How are you?"
> and no one says *How aren't you?*

Rumi advises spiritual window-shoppers to buy something.

> Even if you don't know what you want,
> buy *something*, to be part of the exchanging flow.
> Start a huge, foolish project,
> like Noah.

These last two lines are only a translation, and yet there is a very beautiful progression of vowel sounds, in which *huge* and *foolish* provide a base, and then the *ah* of *project* leads on to the satisfaction of the *O* in *Noah*. The translation ends with two lines whose sequence of pitches is absolutely accurate to the way we say things:

> It makes absolutely no difference
> what people think of you.

Certain colloquial phrases allow complicated ideas to be said very briefly. The Sufi tradition contains the idea that each of our souls has come down here from some other place and will, like the Prodigal Son, eventually develop a desire to go back:

> My soul is from elsewhere, I'm sure of that,
> and I intend to end up there.

> This drunkenness began in some other tavern.
> When I get back around to that place,
> I'll be completely sober.

In the Persian tradition the wine that is spoken of is not actual wine, but the wine of ecstasy. So there's a great charm in saying, "This drunkenness began in some other tavern."

Love Dogs

RUMI

One night a man was crying,
                    Allah! Allah!
His lips grew sweet with the praising,
until a cynic said,
                    "So! I have heard you
calling out, but have you ever
gotten any response?"

The man had no answer to that.
He quit praying and fell into a confused sleep.

He dreamed he saw Khidr, the guide of souls,
in a thick, green foliage.
                    "Why did you stop praising?"
"Because I've never heard anything back."
                    "This longing
you express *is* the return message."

The grief you cry out from
draws you toward union.

Your pure sadness
that wants help
is the secret cup.

Listen to the moan of a dog for its master.
That whining is the connection.

There are love-dogs
no one knows the names of.

Give your life
to be one of them.

Translated by Coleman Barks

Say Yes Quickly

RUMI

Forget your life. Say *God is Great*. Get up.
You think you know what time it is. It's time to pray.
You've carved so many little figurines, too many.
Don't knock on any random door like a beggar.
Reach your long hand out to another door, beyond where
you go on the street, the street
where everyone says, "How are you?"
and no one says *How aren't you?*

Tomorrow you'll see what you've broken and torn tonight,
thrashing in the dark. Inside you
there's an artist you don't know about.
He's not interested in how things look different in moon-
      light.

If you are here unfaithfully with us,
you're causing terrible damage.
If you've opened your loving to God's love,
you're helping people you don't know
and have never seen.

Is what I say true? Say *yes* quickly,
if you know, if you've known it
from before the beginning of the universe.

Translated by Coleman Barks

The Instruments

RUMI

Who is the luckiest in this whole orchestra? The reed.
Its mouth touches your lips to learn music.

All reeds, sugarcane especially, think only
of this chance. They sway in the canebrakes,
free in the many ways they dance.

Without you the instruments would die.
One sits close beside you. Another takes a long kiss.
The tambourine begs, *Touch my skin so I can be myself.*

Let me feel you enter each limb bone by bone,
that what died last night can be whole today.

Why live some soberer way, and feel you ebbing out?
I won't do it.

Either give me enough wine or leave me alone,
now that I know how it is
to be with you in a constant conversation.

Translated by Coleman Barks

On Resurrection Day

RUMI

On Resurrection Day your body testifies against you.
Your hand says, "I stole money."
Your lips, "I said meanness."
Your feet, "I went where I shouldn't."
Your genitals, "Me too."

They will make your praying sound hypocritical.
Let the body's doings speak openly now,
without your saying a word,
as a student's walking behind a teacher
says, "This one knows more clearly
than I the way."

Translated by Coleman Barks

I Have Such a Teacher

RUMI

Last night my teacher taught me the lesson of Poverty:
Having nothing and wanting nothing.

I am a naked man standing inside a mine of rubies,
clothed in red silk.
I absorb the shining and now I see the ocean,
billions of simultaneous motions
moving in me.
A circle of lovely, quiet people
becomes the ring on my finger.

Then the wind and thunder of rain on the way.
I have such a teacher.

Translated by Coleman Barks

These spiritual windowshoppers

RUMI

These spiritual windowshoppers,
who idly ask, *How much is that? Oh, I'm just looking.*
They handle a hundred items and put them down,
shadows with no capital.

What is spent is love and two eyes wet with weeping.
But these walk into a shop,
and their whole lives pass suddenly in that moment,
in that shop.

Where did you go? "Nowhere."
What did you have to eat? "Nothing much."

Even if you don't know what you want,
buy *something,* to be part of the exchanging flow.

Start a huge, foolish project,
like Noah.

It makes absolutely no difference
what people think of you.

Translated by Coleman Barks

Who Says Words with My Mouth?

RUMI

All day I think about it, then at night I say it.
Where did I come from, and what am I supposed to be do-
    ing?
I have no idea.
My soul is from elsewhere, I'm sure of that,
and I intend to end up there.

This drunkenness began in some other tavern.
When I get back around to that place,
I'll be completely sober. Meanwhile,
I'm like a bird from another continent, sitting in this aviary.
The day is coming when I fly off,
but who is it now in my ear, who hears my voice?
Who says words with my mouth?

Who looks out with my eyes? What is the soul?
I cannot stop asking.
If I could taste one sip of an answer,
I could break out of this prison for drunks.
I didn't come here of my own accord, and I can't leave that
    way.
Let whoever brought me here take me back.

This poetry. I never know what I'm going to say.
I don't plan it.
When I'm outside the saying of it,
I get very quiet and rarely speak at all.

Translated by Coleman Barks

A chickpea leaps

RUMI

A chickpea leaps almost over the rim of the pot
where it's being boiled.

"Why are you doing this to me?"

The cook knocks it down with the ladle.

"Don't you try to jump out.
You think I'm torturing you,
I'm giving you flavor,
so you can mix with spices and rice
and be the lovely vitality of a human being.

Remember when you drank rain in the garden.
That was for this."

Grace first. Sexual pleasure,
then a boiling new life begins,
and the Friend has something good to eat.

Translated by Coleman Barks

The Force of Friendship
RUMI

A sea-cow, a dugong, finds a special pearl
and brings it up on land at night. By the light it gives off
the dugong can graze on hyacinths and lilies.

The excrement of the dugong is precious ambergris
because it eats such beauty. Anyone who feeds on Majesty
becomes eloquent. The bee, from mystic inspiration,
fills its rooms with honey.

So the dugong grazes at night in the pearl-glow.
Presently, a merchant comes and drops black loam
over the pearl, then hides behind a tree to watch.

The dugong surges about the meadow like a blind bull.
Twenty times it rushes at nothing, passing the mound
where the pearl is.
                    So Satan couldn't see
the spirit-center inside Adam.
                              God says, *Descend,*
and a huge pearl from Aden gets buried under dirt.
The merchant knows,
                    but the dugong doesn't.

Every clay-pile with a pearl inside
loves to be near any other clay-pile with a pearl,
but those without pearls cannot stand to be near
the hidden companionship.

Remember the mouse on the riverbank?
There's a love-string stretching into the water
hoping for the frog.
                    Suddenly a raven grips the mouse
and flies off. The frog too, from the riverbottom,
with one foot tangled in invisible string,
follows, suspended in the air.
                              Amazed faces ask,
When did a raven ever go underwater
                              and catch a frog?

The frog answers,
                    "This is the force of Friendship."
What draws Friends together
does not conform to Laws of Nature.
Form doesn't know about spiritual closeness.
If a grain of barley approaches a grain of wheat,
an ant must be carrying it. A black ant on black felt.
You can't see it, but if grains go toward each other,
it's there.
              A hand shifts our birdcages around.
Some are brought closer. Some move apart.
Do not try to reason it out. Be conscious
of who draws you and who not.

Gabriel was always there with Jesus, lifting him
above the dark-blue vault, the night-fortress world,
just as the raven of longing carries the flying frog.

                              Translated by Coleman Barks

Someone Digging in the Ground
RUMI

An eye is meant to see things.
The soul is here for its own joy.
A head has one use: For loving a true love.
Legs: To run after.

Love is for vanishing into the sky. The mind,
for learning what men have done and tried to do.
Mysteries are not to be solved. The eye goes blind
when it only wants to see *why*.

A lover is always accused of something.
But when he finds his love, whatever was lost
in the looking comes back completely changed.
On the way to Mecca, many dangers: Thieves,
the blowing sand, only camel's milk to drink.
Still, each pilgrim kisses the black stone there
with pure longing, feeling in the surface
the taste of the lips he wants.

This talk is like stamping new coins. They pile up,
while the real work is done outside
by someone digging in the ground.

Translated by Coleman Barks

Names

RUMI

You should try to hear the name the Holy One has for
    things.
There is something in the phrase: "The Holy One taught
    him names."
We name everything according to the number of legs it has;
The other one names it according to what is inside.
Moses waved his stick; he thought it was a "rod."
But inside its name was "dragonish snake."
We thought the name of Umar was "agitator against God,"
But in eternity his name is "the one who believes."
No one knows our name until our last breath goes out.

The Edge of the Roof

RUMI

I don't like it here, I want to go back.
According to the old Knowers
If you're absent from the one you love
Even for one second that ruins the whole thing!

There must be someone . . . just to find
One *sign* of the other world in this town
Would be enough.

You know the great Chinese Simurgh bird
Got caught in this net . . .
And what can I do? I'm only a wren.

My desire-body, don't come
Strolling over this way.
Sit where you are, that's a good place.

When you want dessert, you choose something rich.
In wine, you look for what is clear and firm.
What is the rest? The rest is mirages,
And blurry pictures, and milk mixed with water.
The rest is self-hatred, and mocking other people, and
        bombing.

So just be quiet and sit down.
The reason is: you are drunk,
And this is the edge of the roof.

Praising Manners

RUMI

We should ask God
To help us toward manners. Inner gifts
Do not find their way
To creatures without just respect.

If a man or woman flails about, he not only
Smashes his house,
He burns the world down.

Your depression is connected to your insolence
And your refusal to praise. If a man or woman is
On the path, and refuses to praise—that man or woman
Steals from others every day—in fact is a shoplifter!

The sun became full of light when it got hold of itself.
Angels began shining when they achieved discipline.
The sun goes out whenever the cloud of not-praising comes
near.
The moment that foolish angel felt insolent, he heard the
door close.

Eating Poetry

RUMI

My poems resemble the bread of Egypt—one night
Passes over it, and you can't eat it any more.

So gobble them down now, while they're still fresh,
Before the dust of the world settles on them.

Where a poem belongs is here, in the warmth of the chest;
Out in the world it dies of cold.

You've seen a fish—put him on dry land,
He quivers for a few minutes, and then is still.

And even if you eat my poems while they're still fresh,
You still have to bring forward many images yourself.

Actually, friend, what you're eating is your own imagination.
These poems are not just some old sayings and saws.

Idle Questions

RUMI

A person hit a Worker a good strong blow from behind.

The Worker swung around to return it; and the man said:

"Before you hit me, I have a question for you.

Now this is it: that sound: was it made by my hand or your
neck?"

"The pain I am feeling does not give me leave for specula-
tion.

These things are all right to worry about if you're feeling no
pain."

The Mill, the Stone, and the Water

RUMI

All our desire is a grain of wheat.
Our whole personality is the milling-building.
But this mill grinds without knowing about it.

The mill stone is your heavy body.
What makes the stone turn is your thought-river.
The stone says: I don't know why we do all this, but the river
     has knowledge!

If you ask the river, it says,
I don't know why I flow.
All I know is that a human opened the gate!

And if you ask the person, he says:
All I know, oh gobbler of bread, is that if this stone
Stops going around, there'll be no bread for your bread-
     soup!

All this grinding goes on, and no one has any knowledge!
So just be quiet, and one day turn
To God, and say: "What is this about bread-making?"

The Drunkards
RUMI

The drunkards are rolling in slowly, those who hold to wine
   are approaching.
The lovers come, singing, from the garden, the ones with
   brilliant eyes.

The I-don't-want-to-lives are leaving, and the I-want-to-
   lives are arriving.
They have gold sewn into their clothes, sewn in for those
   who have none.

Those with ribs showing who have been grazing in the old
   pasture of love
Are turning up fat and frisky.

The souls of pure teachers are arriving like rays of sunlight
From so far up to the ground-huggers.

How marvellous is that garden, where apples and pears, both
   for the sake of the two Marys,
Are arriving even in winter.

Those apples grow from the Gift, and they sink back into the
   Gift.
It must be that they are coming from the garden to the gar-
   den.

That Journeys Are Good
RUMI

If a fir tree had a foot or two like a turtle, or a wing,
Do you think it would just wait for the saw to enter?

You know the sun journeys all night under the earth;
If it didn't, how could it throw up its flood of light in the
     east?

And salt water climbs with such marvellous swiftness to the
     sky.
If it didn't, how would the cabbages be fed with the rain?

Have you thought of Joseph lately? Didn't he leave his fa-
     ther in tears, going?
Didn't he then learn how to understand dreams, and give
     away grain?

And you, if you can't leave your country, you could go into
     yourself,
And become a ruby mine, open to the gifts of the sun.

You could travel from your manhood into the inner man, or
     from your womanhood into the inner woman—
By a journey of that sort earth became a place where you find
     gold.

So leave your complaints and self-pity and internalized
     death-energy.

Don't you realize how many fruits have already escaped out
of sourness into sweetness?

A good source of sweetness is a teacher; mine is named
Shams.
You know every fruit grows more handsome in the light of
the sun.

Longing for the Birds of Solomon

RUMI

Is this stuff poetry? It's what birds sing in cages.
Where are the words spoken by the birds of Solomon?

How would you know their cries, if you heard them,
When you haven't seen Solomon even for two seconds?

Solomon's bird lifts his wings, one tip touches East, one
 West.
Those who hear the note feel an intensity in their whole
 body.

The bird descends from the Holy One's bedroom door to
 earth.
And from earth it flies among light back to the Great Seat.

Without Solomon every bird is a bat in love with darkness.
Listen, oh mischievous bat, try to become his friend. Do you
 want to stay in your cave forever?

If you go even three feet towards Solomon's mountain,
Others will use that as a yardstick to measure their lives.

Suppose your leg is gimpy, and you have to hop, what's the
 difference?
Going toward Solomon, even by limping, the leg grows
 whole.

The Hawk

RUMI

We are a little crazier now, and less sober, and some joy has
risen out of us . . . it was so glad to be gone . . .

When it noticed the sober watcher no longer was holding its
leg, it flew—

It is not in the mountains nor the marshes, it has sent itself
to be with the Holy One who is alone.

Don't look here and there in the house, it belongs to air,
it is made of air, and has gone into air.

This is a white hawk that belongs to Gawain's master;
it belongs to him and has gone to him.

VIII

Leaving the Body or Entering It?

W hen a person becomes religious, does that person's spirit leave the body? Or finally enter it? The Neoplatonists, Plotinus among them, insist that we have to ascend out of matter in order to achieve the purity that brings us near God. Many others say "No." They say, "Stay in your body and become a lover." They say that God isn't attracted to the perfection in you, but to the fiery lover.

Mirabai, who wrote in Rajasthani in the 13th century, is still adored all over India as a model of the lover poet. During her twenties, her husband, a prince, died in a war; and she decided to go inward. She found a low-born teacher, and at night she would tie her saris together and climb down the castle walls to visit him. Then she would wash his old feet and drink the water. She had learned to live in the Garden. Her family hated all that. Her brother-in-law, Rana, sent her poison one day, and at another time a poisonous snake. She mentions these incidents in her poems.

Through her teacher, she, one could say, became the female divinity Radha. Her marriage then with Radha's lover, Krishna, took place inside her body and also outside in the universe. His face was dark blue in color, suggesting, among other things, the darker-skinned people of South India. He is the One she makes love with in the Garden:

Mira's lord is half lion and half man.
She turns her life over to the midnight of his hair.

Mirabai's tradition of poetry includes six states of religious life. The first is separation from God, which some Christians consider to be a state of sin, but the Hindus call it a holy state like any other. The second is momentary union with the Divine, followed by a renewed separation. Her poems "Don't go, don't go" and "Where did you go?" are written from this second station. Some Indian poets write poems describing only separation, and are still considered religious poets. Mirabai writes poems from all the stations.

The tradition of the Lover ties religious life to music, to poetry, and to dance. We know that Mirabai composed music for her poems—often a separate tune for each line—and that she went from village to village, singing to poems and dancing them. Her poems are still enthusiastically performed.

Vidyapati speaks in some poems as if he were a woman. Vidyapati *is* feminine to God. In "The girl and the woman," he suggests an idea that modern Puritans will find hard to accept: that the woman with abundant sexuality is closest to God. Mahadeviyakka compares the soul to a silkworm who makes a Garden from her own body; and the soul's love is Shiva, "the Lord white as Jasmine." Bibi Hayati Kermani, the Iranian woman who lived last century, continues the tradition of questioning the State we are in:

Is this then the night of power
or is it only your hair?

The heat embodied in the tradition of the Divine Lover gradually pressed westward. Hindi and Persian poetry affected Muslim culture; and Muslim culture affected the Jews and the Christians living with the Muslims in Spain, and virtually created the troubadour poetry in France and Germany.

St. John of the Cross, sitting in prison for his unorthodox thoughts, heard through the window a few bars of a Spanish-Arab love song, and composed his magnificent poem, "The Dark Night," in which the lover's heat, felt so long in Rajasthani, in Hindi, in Persian, in Urdu, in Arabic, appears in Spanish. As we can tell from Emily Dickinson's poem, some of that breath came through to Amherst.

His Hair

MIRABAI

You play the flute well; I love your swing curls and your
    earlocks.
Jasumati, your mother, wasn't she the one
Who washed and combed your beautiful hair?
If you come anywhere near my house,
I will close my sandalwood doors, and lock you in.

Mira's lord is half lion and half man.
She turns her life over to the midnight of his hair.

Don't go, don't go

MIRABAI

Don't go, don't go. I touch your soles. I'm sold to you.
No one knows where to find the bhakti path, show me where
    to go.
I would like my own body to turn into a heap of incense and
    sandalwood
And you set a torch to it.
When I've fallen down to gray ashes, smear me on your
    shoulders and chest.
Mira says: You who lift mountains, I have some light,
    I want to mingle it with yours.

LEAVING THE BODY OR ENTERING IT?

Where did you go?

MIRABAI

Where did you go, Holy One, after you left my body?
Your flame jumped to the wick, and then you disappeared
    and left the lamp alone.
You put the boat into the surf, and then walked inland,
    leaving the boat in the ocean of parting.
Mira says: Tell me when you will come to meet me.

O my friends

MIRABAI

O my friends,
What can you tell me of Love,
Whose pathways are filled with strangeness?
When you offer the Great One your love,
At the first step your body is crushed.
Next be ready to offer your head as his seat.
Be ready to orbit his lamp like a moth giving in to the light,
To live in the deer as she runs toward the hunter's call,
In the partridge that swallows hot coals for love of the moon,
In the fish that, kept from the sea, happily dies.
Like a bee trapped for life in the closing of the sweet flower,
Mira has offered herself to her Lord.
She says: the single Lotus will swallow you whole.

Translated by Jane Hirshfield

I was going to the river for water

MIRABAI

I was going to the river for water,
the gold pitcher balanced with care upon my head,
and Love's knife entered my heart.
Now God has bound me tightly with that fine thread,
he takes me wherever he will.
Mira's Lord is the dark-bodied, beautiful Giridhara.
What he wishes to be, he is.

Translated by Jane Hirshfield

Faithfulness

MIRABAI

My friend, he looked, and our eyes met; an arrow came in.
My chest opened; what could it do? His image moved inside.
I've been standing all morning in the door of my house,
    looking down the road.
The one I love is dark: he is an herb growing in secret places,
    an herb that heals wounds.
Mira says: The town thinks I am loose, but I am faithful to
    the Dark One.

All I Was Doing Was Breathing
MIRABAI

Something has reached out and taken in the beams of my
    eyes.
There is a longing, it is for his body, for every hair of that
    dark body.
All I was doing was being, and the Dancing Energy came by
    my house.
His face looks curiously like the moon, I saw it from the side,
    smiling.
My family says: "Don't ever see him again!" And implies
    things in a low voice.
But my eyes have their own life; they laugh at rules, and
    know whose they are.
I believe I can bear on my shoulders whatever you want to
    say of me.
Mira says: Without the energy that lifts mountains, how am I
    to live?

Ankle Bells

MIRABAI

Mira dances, how can her ankle bells not dance?
"Mira is insane," strangers say that, "the family's ruined."
Poison came to the door one day; she drank it and laughed.
I am at Hari's feet; I give him body and soul.
A glimpse of him is water: How thirsty I am for that!
Mira's Lord is the one who lifts mountains, he removes evil
    from human life.
Mira's Lord attacks the beings of greed; for safety I go to
    him.

LEAVING THE BODY OR ENTERING IT?

Why Mira Can't Go Back to Her Old House
MIRABAI

The colors of the Dark One have penetrated Mira's body; all
the other colors washed out.
Making love with the Dark One and eating little, those are
my pearls and my carnelians.
Meditation beads and the forehead streak, those are my
scarves and my rings.
That's enough feminine wiles for me. My teacher taught me
this.
Approve me or disapprove me: I praise the Mountain Energy
night and day.
I take the path that ecstatic human beings have taken for
centuries.
I don't steal money, I don't hit anyone. What will you charge
me with?
I have felt the swaying of the elephant's shoulders; and now
you want me to climb on a jackass? Try to be serious.

The Clouds
MIRABAI

When I saw the dark clouds, I wept, Oh Dark One, I wept at
the dark clouds.
Black clouds soared up, and took some yellow along; rain
did fall, some rain fell long.
There was water east of the house, west of the house; fields
all green.
The one I love lives past those fields; rain has fallen on my
body, on my hair, as I wait in the open door for him.
The Energy that holds up mountains is the energy Mirabai
bows down to.
He lives century after century, and the test I set for him he
has passed.

It's True I Went to the Market
MIRABAI

My friend, I went to the market and bought the Dark One.
You claim by night, I say by day.
Actually I was beating a drum all the time I was buying him.
You say I gave too much; I say too little.
Actually, I put him on a scale before I bought him.
What I paid was my social body, my town body, my family
body, and all my inherited jewels.
Mirabai says: The Dark One is my husband now.
Be with me when I lie down; you promised me this in an
earlier life.

LEAVING THE BODY OR ENTERING IT?

The Music

MIRABAI

My friend, the stain of the Great Dancer has penetrated my
  body.
I drank the cup of music, and I am hopelessly drunk.
Moreover I stay drunk, no matter what I do to become sober.
Rana, who disapproves, gave me one basket with a snake in
  it.
Mira folded the snake around her neck, it was a lover's
  bracelet, lovely!
Rana's next gift was poison: "This is something for you,
  Mira."
She repeated the Holy Name in her chest, and drank it, it was
  good!
Every name He has is praise; that's the cup I like to drink,
  and only that.
"The Great Dancer is my husband," Mira says, "rain washes
  off all the other colors."

The Coffer with the Poisonous Snake

MIRABAI

Rana sent a gold coffer of complicated ivory;
But inside a black and green asp was waiting,
"It is a necklace that belonged to a great Queen!"
I put it around my neck; it fit well.
It became a string of lovely pearls, each with a moon inside.
My room then was full of moonlight as if the full moon
Had found its way in through the open window.

The Heat of Midnight Tears

MIRABAI

Listen, my friend, this road is the heart opening,
Kissing his feet, resistance broken, tears all night.

If we could reach the Lord through immersion in water,
I would have asked to be born a fish in this life.
If we could reach Him through nothing but berries and wild
    nuts
Then surely the saints would have been monkeys when they
    came from the womb!
If we could reach him by munching lettuce and dry leaves
Then the goats would surely get to the Holy One before us!

If the worship of stone statues could bring us all the way,
I would have adored a granite mountain years ago.

Mirabai says: The heat of midnight tears will bring you to
    God.

LEAVING THE BODY OR ENTERING IT?

When Do I Join You?

MAHADEVIYAKKA

Like a silkworm weaving
her house with love
from her marrow,
                    and dying
in her body's threads
winding tight, round
and round,
                    I burn
desiring what the heart desires.

Cut through, O lord,
my heart's greed,
and show me
your way out,

O lord white as jasmine.

Till you've earned
knowledge of good and evil

   it is
   lust's body,
   site of rage,
   ambush of greed,
   house of passion,
   fence of pride,
   mask of envy.

Till you know and lose this knowing

you've no way
of knowing
my lord white as jasmine.

Like an elephant
lost from his herd
suddenly captured,

remembering his mountains,
   his Vindhyas,
      I remember.

A parrot
come into a cage
remembering his mate,
   I remember.

O lord white as jasmine
show me
your ways.
   Call me: Child, come here,
      come this way.

Riding the blue sapphire mountains
wearing moonstone for slippers
blowing long horns
O Śiva
when shall I
crush you on my pitcher breasts

   O lord white as jasmine
   when do I join you

195

LEAVING THE BODY OR ENTERING IT?

stripped of body's shame
and heart's modesty?

Translated by A. K. Ramanujan

The sea moves around sea-creatures
VIDYAPATI

The sea moves around sea-creatures,
moonlight around the moon-bird,
the friendly dark around the stars,
my feelings around the Dark One.

In a mirror a face is reversed.
It hungers for the right face,
as my body longs for his.

The rabbit who lives on the moon
leaves a floating stain on its light.
His life is a darkness in mine.

Suppose the sun did not rise at all,
no green tree or pond took on color.
Inside my chest I am night with him gone.

Vidyapati says: My darling, I can tell you
you are marvellously lucky.

The girl and the woman

VIDYAPATI

The girl and the woman breathe together:
the girl lifts her hair on top of her head;
the woman lets it fall over her breasts.

The girl stretches out her naked arms,
and the boldness of her long legs.
The woman throws her sari over both;
She lets fall a faint veil over her own curious look.
Her feet do not remain still;
there is a faint reddening of the breasts;
all is not calm inside.
Behind the darkened lids of her eyes the god's energy
wakes up, flies around
in the bodiless world.

Vidyapati says: Listen to me, oh Holy One,
in a little while this woman will come to you.

LEAVING THE BODY OR ENTERING IT?

The soul, like the moon

LALLA

The soul, like the moon,
is new, and always new again.

And I have seen the ocean
continuously creating.

Since I scoured my mind
and my body, I too, Lalla,
am new, each moment new.

My teacher told me one thing,
Live in the soul.

When that was so,
I began to go naked,
and dance.

Translated by Coleman Barks

Ghazal 96

BIBI HAYATI KERMANI

Is this then the night of power
Or is it only your hair?
Is this dawn or your face?
In the Thesaurus of Beauty
Is this an immortal ode?
Or is it only a floating couplet
Composed by your eyebrow?

Is this moment a useful tree
Or a cypress from the rose garden?
Is this the tree that bears dates in Paradise
Or your own slender and tender form?

Is it the musk carried by Chinese deer
Or the faint rose of rosewater?
Is this the breath the rose breathes
Or the implications of your perfume?

Is this lightning that burns forests
Or a bonfire on Mt. Sana'i?
Is it a painful sigh of mine
Or the true being that you are?

Is this some scent from Mongolia
Or is it ambergris with no defect?
Is this a single hair, curling,
Or your whole head of hair in braids?

Is this the dawn's red wine
Or the magic that we call white?

LEAVING THE BODY OR ENTERING IT?

Is this your eye rolling towards Heaven
Or the sorcerer's glance that makes illusions?

Is this the Garden of Eden
Or a good garden on earth?
Is this a Black Stone the saints
Loved, or an alley behind your house?

Praying, we all turn our face to a holy
Building made of mud and straw.
Hayati's has a holy
Building turned towards your face.

Translated by Adam Harcani

The Shulamite

ELSE LASKER-SCHÜLER

O, from your sweet mouth I have come
To know beatitude so well!
Already I feel the lips of Gabriel
Burning on my breast . . .
And the night-clouds drink
My deep dream of cedars.
O, how your life beckons me!
And I vanish
With flowering heartache,
I blow away into space,
Into time,
To forever,
And my soul burns away in the evening colors
of Jerusalem.

Translated by Robert Alter

LEAVING THE BODY OR ENTERING IT?

Wild Nights—Wild Nights!

EMILY DICKINSON

Wild Nights—Wild Nights!
Were I with thee
Wild Nights should be
Our luxury!

Futile—the Winds—
To a Heart in port—
Done with the Compass—
Done with the Chart!

Rowing in Eden—
Ah, the Sea!
Might I but moor—Tonight—
In Thee!

The Dark Night

ST. JOHN OF THE CROSS

In the night that was dark,
Made fiery by the furies of love
—Oh blesséd moment!—
I left without being noticed,
All the doors of my house closed for the night.

Secure and in the dark,
On the secret staircase, stealth
—Oh blesséd moment!—
And darkness protected me,
All the doors of my house closed for the night.

In the delicious night,
In privacy, where no one saw me,
Nor did I see one thing,
I had no light or guide
But the fire that burned inside my chest.

That fire showed me
The way more clearly than the blaze of noon
To where, waiting for me,
Was the One I knew so well,
In that place where no one ever is.

Oh night, sweet guider,
Oh night more marvelous than dawn!
Oh night which joins
The lover and the beloved
So that the lover and beloved change bodies!

LEAVING THE BODY OR ENTERING IT?

In my chest full of flowers,
Flowering wholly and only for Him,
There He remained sleeping;
I cared for Him there,
And the fan of the high cedars cooled Him.

The wind played with
His hair, and that wind from the high
Towers struck me on the neck
With its sober hand;
Sight, taste, touch, hearing stopped.

I stood still; I forgot who I was,
My face leaning against Him,
Everything stopped, abandoned me,
My worldliness was gone, forgotten
Among the white lilies.

IX

Dying To This World

The theme of this group of poems is one characteristic of all religious life, namely, giving up a love of this world. Giving up love of this world may be death to the Nafs, but it is life to the spirit. So some writers say you have to get used to the Nafs's fear of dying. Goethe says:

And so long as you haven't experienced
This: to die and so to grow,
You are only a troubled guest
On the dark earth.

The Buddhist poet Dogen has full confidence that the soul, having arrived here on its own, will be able to find its way back:

The migrating bird
leaves no trace behind
and does not need a guide.

Margaret of Navarre, who belonged to that miraculous group of Provençal poets, trained herself to give up love of this world by saying, "Wind will blow it all away":

And if they next, to make
You less open to God,
Say (to flatter you)
That you are truly great:
    Turn your back
    To talk of that sort.
Wind will blow it all away.

Gerard Manley Hopkins in "The Windhover" gives magnificent praise to the falcon for his enormously heroic flight on the "rolling level underneath him steady air." But even more beautiful, Hopkins says, are the colors we see when burning logs break into embers and fall:

> . . . blue-bleak embers, ah my dear,
> Fall, gall themselves, and gash gold-vermilion.

Emily Dickinson compares the person able to give up comforts to the hemlock:

> I think the Hemlock likes to stand
> Upon a Marge of Snow—
>
> The Hemlock's nature thrives—on cold—
> The Gnash of Northern winds
> Is sweetest nutriment—to him—

Marvell's poetry on this theme is strong and witty. He says that the body likes it here and is very angry that the soul gives it so many tortures and disciplines. The soul replies that it has to endure diseases:

> . . . but, what's worse, the cure;
> And ready oft the port to gain,
> Am shipwrecked into health again.

The Holy Longing

JOHANN WOLFGANG VON GOETHE

Tell a wise person, or else keep silent,
Because the massman will mock it right away.
I praise what is truly alive,
What longs to be burned to death.

In the calm water of the love-nights,
Where you were begotten, where you have begotten,
A strange feeling comes over you
When you see the silent candle burning.

Now you are no longer caught
In the obsession with darkness,
And a desire for higher love-making
Sweeps you upward.

Distance does not make you falter,
Now, arriving in magic, flying,
And, finally, insane for the light,
You are the butterfly and you are gone.

And so long as you haven't experienced
This: to die and so to grow,
You are only a troubled guest
On the dark earth.

The Second Poem the Night-Walker Wrote
JOHANN WOLFGANG VON GOETHE

Over all the hilltops
Silence,
Among all the treetops
You feel hardly
A breath moving.
The birds fall silent in the woods.
Simply wait! Soon
You too will be silent.

Coming or Going
DOGEN

The migrating bird
leaves no trace behind
and does not need a guide.

To the Tree-Brother with a Few Days Left
RENÉ CHAR

Small harp of the larch trees,
On the buttress made of moss and growing flagstones,
—edge of the forests where the cloud breaks—
Resonating note of the emptiness, in which I believe.

The Windhover

GERARD MANLEY HOPKINS

To Christ Our Lord

I caught this morning morning's minion, king-
   dom of daylight's dauphin, dapple-dawn-drawn Falcon,
   in his riding
     Of the rolling level underneath him steady air, and
     striding
High there, how he rung upon the rein of a wimpling wing
In his ecstasy! then off, off forth on swing,
   As a skate's heel sweeps smooth on a bow-bend: the hurl
   and gliding
Rebuffed the big wind. My heart in hiding
Stirred for a bird,—the achieve of, the mastery of the thing!

Brute beauty and valour and act, oh, air, pride, plume, here
Buckle! AND the fire that breaks from thee then, a billion
Times told lovelier, more dangerous, O my chevalier!

No wonder of it: shéer plód makes plough down sillion
Shine, and blue-bleak embers, ah my dear,
   Fall, gall themselves, and gash gold-vermilion.

must an
even the most
eloquent

Bread and Wine, Part 7

FRIEDRICH HÖLDERLIN

Oh friend, we arrived too late. The divine energies
  Are still alive, but isolated above us, in the archetypal
    world.
They keep on going there, and, apparently, don't bother if
  Humans live or not . . . that is a heavenly mercy.
Sometimes a human's clay is not strong enough to take the
    water;
  Human beings can carry the divine only sometimes.
What is living now? Night dreams of them. But craziness
  Helps, so does sleep. Grief and Night toughen us,
Until people capable of sacrifice once more rock
  In the iron cradle, desire people, as the ancients, strong
    enough for water.
In thunderstorms it will arrive. I have the feeling often,
    meanwhile,
  It is better to sleep, since the Guest comes so seldom;
We waste our life waiting, and I haven't the faintest idea
  How to act or talk . . . in the lean years who needs poets? *
But poets as you say are like the holy disciple of the Wild
    One
  Who used to stroll over the fields through the whole di-
    vine night.

* When do you need poets more?

A Dialogue between God and the Soul

GEORGE HERBERT

Love bade me welcome: yet my soul drew back,
　　Guiltie of dust and sinne.
But quick-ey'd Love, observing me grow slack
　　From my first entrance in,
Drew nearer to me, sweetly questioning
　　If I lack'd any thing.

'A guest,' I answer'd, 'worthy to be here':
　　Love said, 'You shall be he.'
'I the unkinde, ungratefull? Ah, my deare,
　　I cannot look on thee.'
Love took my hand, and smiling did reply,
　　'Who made the eyes but I?'

'Truth Lord, but I have marr'd them: let my shame
　　Go where it doth deserve.'
'And know you not,' sayes Love, 'who bore the blame?'
　　'My deare, then I will serve.'
'You must sit down,' sayes Love, 'and taste my meat':
　　So I did sit and eat.　← The greatest love,
　　　　　　　　　The greatest humility

I came to love you too late

ST. AUGUSTINE

I came to love you too late, Oh Beauty, so ancient and so new. Yes, I came to love you too late. What did I know? You were inside me, and I was out of my body and mind, looking for you. I drove like an ugly madman against the beautiful things and beings you made. You were in fact inside me, but I was not inside you. Those same things kept me at some distance from you, even though those things, had they not been inside you, would not have existed at all. You called to me and cried to me; you broke the bowl of my deafness; you uncovered your beams, and threw them at me; you rejected my blindness; you blew a fragrant wind on me, and I sucked in my breath and wanted you; I tasted you and now I want you as I want food and water; you touched me, and I have been burning ever since to have your peace.

The Hole in the Basket

BHARTRIHARI

A mouse once gnawed a hole in a basket
In which a famished snake lay sleeping.
The mouse fell into the snake's open mouth.
Then the snake, revived by his meal,
Crawled out through the same hole
By which the mouse entered.
Friends, be satisfied with your life!
You'll never understand why
One person rises and another falls.

Leave me, O Love

SIR PHILIP SIDNEY

Leave me, O Love, which reachest but to dust;
And thou, my mind, aspire to higher things;
Grow rich in that which never taketh rust,
Whatever fades but fading pleasure brings.
Draw in thy beams, and humble all thy might
To that sweet yoke where lasting freedoms be;
Which breaks the clouds and opens forth the light,
That doth both shine and give us sight to see.
Oh, take fast hold; let that light be thy guide
In this small course which birth draws out to death,
And think how evil becometh him to slide,
Who seeketh heaven, and comes of heavenly breath.
   Then farewell, world; thy uttermost I see;
   Eternal Love, maintain thy life in me.

A Dialogue between the Soul and Body

ANDREW MARVELL

SOUL

Oh, who shall from this dungeon raise
A soul enslaved so many ways?
With bolts of bones, that fettered stands
In feet, and manacled in hands;
Here blinded with an eye and there
Deaf with the drumming of an ear;
A soul hung up, as 'twere, in chains
Of nerves and arteries and veins;
Tortured, besides each other part,
In a vain head and double heart.

BODY

Oh, who shall me deliver whole
From bonds of this tyrannic soul?
Which stretched upright, impales me so
That mine own precipice I go;
And warms and moves this needless frame,
A fever could but do the same.
And, wanting where its spite to try,
Has made me live to let me die.
A body that could never rest,
Since this ill spirit it possessed.

SOUL

What magic could me thus confine
Within another's grief to pine,
Where whatsoever it complain,
I feel, that cannot feel, the pain?

And all my care itself employs,
That to preserve which me destroys.
Constrained not only to endure
Diseases, but, what's worse, the cure;
And ready oft the port to gain,
Am shipwrecked into health again.

BODY
But physic yet could never reach
The maladies thou me dost teach:
Whom first the cramp of hope does tear,
And then the palsy shakes of fear;
The pestilence of love does heat,
Or hatred's hidden ulcer eat.
Joy's cheerful madness does perplex,
Or sorrow's other madness vex;
Which knowledge forces me to know,
And memory will not forego.
What but a soul could have the wit
To build me up for sin so fit?
So architects do square and hew
Green trees that in the forest grew.

Daybreak

GALWAY KINNELL

On the tidal mud, just before sunset,
dozens of starfishes
were creeping. It was
as though the mud were a sky
and enormous, imperfect stars
moved across it as slowly
as the actual stars cross heaven.
All at once they stopped,
and as if they had simply
increased their receptivity
to gravity they sank down
into the mud; they faded down
into it and lay still; and by the time
pink of sunset broke across them
they were as invisible
as the true stars at daybreak.

DYING TO THIS WORLD

from *Praise for Death*

DONALD HALL

I

Let us praise death that turns pink cheeks to ashes,
that reduces father from son and daughter, that sets tears
in the tall widow's eye. Let us praise death that gathers
us loose-limbed and weeping by the grave's edge in the flat
yard near the sea that continues. Let us praise death

2

that fastens my body to yours and renders skin
against skin sometimes intolerably sweet, as October
sweetens the flesh of a McIntosh apple. Let us praise
death that prints snapshots, fixing an afternoon forty
years ago on a sandy lane. While we stand holding

3

each other, let us praise death as a dog praises
its master, bowing, paying obeisance, rolling over;
let us praise death as a spaniel praises a pitbull.
What remained of her at the end, compared to my friend
eight months before, was the orange peel to the orange:

4

as if the shard of fruit—once pungent and moist, now
    smeared
with coffeegrounds—pulsed, opened an eye, and screamed
without stopping. As we enter the passage of agony,
imagining darkness prepared underground, we recollect
Jesus who drank from the cup: "Why have you forsaken
    me?"

33
Let us praise death in old age. Wagging our tails,
bowing, whimpering, let us praise sudden crib-death
and death in battle: Dressed in blue the rifleman charges
the granite wall. Let us praise airplane crashes.
We buried thirty-year-old Stephen the photographer

34
in Michigan's November rain. His bony widow Sarah, pale
in her loose black dress, leaned forward impulsively
as the coffin, suspended from a yellow crane, swayed
over the hole. When she touched the shiny damp maple
of the box, it swung slightly away from her

35
as it continued downward. Stephen's mother Joan
knelt first to scrape wet dirt onto the coffin lid;
then his father Peter lifted handfuls and let them drop,
then his sister Sarah, then his widow Sarah. Under
scraggly graveyard trees, five young gravediggers stood

36
smoking together, men tattooed and unshaven, wearing
baseball caps, shifting from foot to foot, saying
nothing, trying never to watch in Michigan's November
    rain.
"Bitterly, bitterly I weep for my blood-brother Enkidu.
Should I *praise* master death that commanded my friend?

37
"I wander hunting in the forest weeping salt tears;
in my anger I slaughter the deer. Bitterly I cry:

DYING TO THIS WORLD

'Nowhere can I lay my head down to rest or to sleep!
Despair sucks my liver out! Desolation eats bitter meat
from my thigh! What happened to my brother will happen to
      me.'

38
"I stood by his body eight days. I implored him to throw
death over, to rise and pull his gold breastplate on.
On the ninth day worms crawled from the skin of his neck.
Now, therefore, I climb to the sun's garden, to Utnapishtim
who alone of all men after the flood lives without dying."

Glory to thee, my God, this night

THOMAS KEN

Glory to thee, my God, this night
For all the blessings of the light;
Keep me, O keep me, King of kings,
Beneath thy own almighty wings.

Forgive me, Lord, for thy dear Son,
The ill that I this day have done,
That with the world, myself, and thee
I, 'ere I sleep, at peace may be.

Teach me to live, that I may dread
The grave as little as my bed;
Teach me to die, that so I may
Rise glorious at the awful day.

O may my soul on thee repose,
And with sweet sleep mine eyelids close,
Sleep that may me more vigorous make
To serve my God when I awake.

When in the night I sleepless lie,
My soul with heavenly thoughts supply;
Let no ill dreams disturb my rest,
No powers of darkness me molest.

Praise God, from whom all blessings flow,
Praise him, all creatures here below,
Praise him above, ye heavenly host,
Praise Father, Son, and Holy Ghost.

The Old Lutheran Bells at Home

WALLACE STEVENS

These are the voices of the pastors calling
In the names of St. Paul and of the halo-John
And of other holy and learned men, among them

Great choristers, propounders of hymns, trumpeters,
Jerome and the scrupulous Francis and Sunday women,
The nurses of the spirit's innocence.

These are the voices of the pastors calling
Much rough-end being to smooth Paradise,
Spreading out fortress walls like fortress wings.

Deep in their sound the stentor Martin sings.
Dark Juan looks outward through his mystic brow.
Each sexton has his sect. The bells have none.

These are the voices of the pastors calling
And calling like the long echoes in long sleep,
Generations of shepherds to generations of sheep.

Each truth is a sect though no bells ring for it.
And the bells belong to the sextons, after all,
As they jangle and dangle and kick their feet.

Roll Call

WILLIAM STAFFORD

Red Wolf came, and Passenger Pigeon,
the Dodo Bird, all the gone or endangered
came and crowded around in a circle,
the Bison, the Irish Elk, waited
silent, the Great White Bear, fluid and strong,
sliding from the sea, streaming and creeping
in the gathering darkness, nose down,
bowing to earth its tapered head,
where the Black-footed Ferret, paws folded,
stood in the center surveying the multitude
and spoke for us all: "Dearly beloved," it said.

Merlin's Riddling

ALFRED, LORD TENNYSON, *THE COMING OF ARTHUR*

Rain, rain, and sun! a rainbow in the sky!
A young man will be wiser by and by
And old man's wit may wander ere he die.
Rain, rain, and sun! a rainbow on the lea!
And truth is this to me, and that to thee;
And truth or clothed or naked let it be.
Rain, sun, and rain! and the free blossom blows:
Sun, rain, and sun! and where is he who knows?
From the great deep to the great deep he goes.

I think the Hemlock

EMILY DICKINSON

I think the Hemlock likes to stand
Upon a Marge of Snow—
It suits his own Austerity—
And satisfies an awe.

That men, must slake in Wilderness—
And in the Desert—cloy—
An instinct for the Hoar, the Bald—
Lapland's—necessity—

The Hemlock's nature thrives—on cold—
The Gnash of Northern winds
Is sweetest nutriment—to him—
His best Norwegian Wines—

To satin Races—he is nought—
But Children on the Don,
Beneath his Tabernacles, play,
And Dnieper Wrestlers, run.

Wind Will Blow It All Away
MARGARET OF NAVARRE

If someone insults you,
Go on, with light heart;
If they *all* do it, pay
No heed to what they say.
   There's no new art
   In talk of that kind.
Wind will blow it all away.

If someone praises Devotion
Implying of course it's OK,
But says of course the works
Of the Law are much greater,
   It's weird dogma,
     Pass by, don't bother.
Wind will blow it all away.

And if they next, to make
You less open to God,
Say (to flatter you)
That you are truly great:
   Turn your back
   To talk of that sort.
Wind will blow it all away.

And if the world itself
Should come, money, castles,
Great sweets in its hand, just say,
"I have enough today."
   For worldly things

Return whence they came.
Wind will blow it all away.

And if people name a place
(Not God's) where all sorrow
Will be settled, all be saved,
They have an evil aim.
  Be strong, say no
  To these odd people.
Wind will blow it all away.

X

*The Spirit—Who Is a Guest
of the Soul—Will Never Be
at Home on This Earth*

Hafez, the Sufi poet, was born in 1320, one hundred and thirteen years after Rumi, in Shiraz in southeast Iran. We know that Hafez was married and had children. His name means "someone who has memorized the entire Koran," and he apparently made his living as a reciter of the Koran. His poems were and are famous for their exquisite form, like a jewel of many faces. In some poems he repeats a single idea in every stanza, such as "Do not sink into sadness," or repeats a verb such as "return." Like other poets, he rhymes sounds; but one could say also that, in an amazing way, he rhymes ideas or feelings.

Often in the Sufi tradition, a distinction is made between the soul and the spirit. The soul is the intelligence that praises this world's beauty—its roses, its wine, its beautiful women and men, its poems and its prayers. The soul is a grateful guest of the earth. The spirit is imagined as a guest of the soul, who is constantly trying to leave.

Hafez is speaking for the soul when he says:

This meadow is composing a tale of a spring day in May;
The serious man lets the future go and accepts the cash now.

Hafez is speaking for the soul again when he says:

The Sultan of Pre-Eternity gave us the casket of love's grief
    as a gift;
Therefore we have turned our sorrow toward this dilapi-
    dated traveller's cabin that we call "the world."

But he is speaking for the spirit when he says:

> From now on I will leave no doors in my heart open for love
>   of beautiful creatures;
> I have turned and set the seal of divine lips on the door of this
>   house.

Later in the poem he says:

> We have turned our face to the pearl lying on the ocean floor.
> So why then should we worry if this wobbly old boat keeps
>   going or not?

These distinctions are passionately held and so difficult that none of us can really understand them. I don't understand them. But we know what they say: the soul is at home on the earth and the spirit visits. It's important that when we look into the basket, we don't cry out, "Oh, there's nothing in the basket!" We know what will happen if we say that.

Night and Sleep

RUMI

At the time of night-prayer, as the sun slides down,
The route the senses walk on closes, the route to the invisible
  opens.

The angel of sleep then gathers and drives along the spirits;
Just as the mountain keeper gathers his sheep on a slope.

And what amazing sights he offers to the descending sheep!
Cities with sparkling streets, hyacinth gardens, emerald
  pastures!

The spirit sees astounding beings, turtles turned to men,
Men turned to angels, when sleep erases the banal.

I think one could say the spirit goes back to its old home;
It no longer remembers where it lives, and loses its fatigue.

It carries around in life so many griefs and loads
And trembles under their weight; they are gone, it is all well.

The Jar with the Dry Rim

RUMI

The mind is an ocean . . . and so many worlds
Are rolling there, mysterious, dimly seen!
And our bodies? Our body is a cup, floating
On the ocean; soon it will fill, and sink. . . .
Not even one bubble will show where it went down.

The spirit is so near that you can't see it!
But reach for it . . . Don't be a jar
Full of water, whose rim is always dry.
Don't be the rider who gallops all night
And never sees the horse that is beneath him.

The Newborn
ATTAR

Muhammed spoke to his friends
about a newborn baby, "This child
may cry out in its helplessness,
but it doesn't want to go back
to the darkness of the womb.

And so it is with your soul
when it finally leaves the nest
and flies out into the sky
over the wide plain of a new life.
Your soul would not trade that freedom
for the warmth of where it was.

Let loving lead your soul.
Make it a place to retire to,
a kind of monastery cave, a retreat
for the deepest core of being.

Then build a road
from there to God.

Let every action be in harmony with your soul
and its soul-place, but don't parade
those doings down the street
on the end of a stick!

Keep quiet and secret with soul-work.
Don't worry so much about your body.
God sewed that robe. Leave it as is.

Be more deeply courageous.
Change your soul."

Translated by Coleman Barks

When the one I love

HAFEZ

When the one I love accepts the wine,
Then the time of the false idols is over.

Whoever looks into his luminous eyes
Cries: "Someone will soon be drunk; get the police!"

I have fallen like a fish into deep water
So that the One I love will throw his net.

I have dropped in a heap on the earth,
Perhaps I will feel a touch on my hand.

How blessed is the man who like Hafez
Has tasted in his heart the wine made before Adam.

The Lost Daughter

HAFEZ

Send out the criers, go to the marketplace of souls,
"Hear, hear, all you in the colonnade of lovers, here it is:

The wild daughter has been reported lost for several days.
Call all your friends! Whoever's near her is in danger.

Her dress is ruby-colored; her hair is done in seafoam;
She takes away reason; be alert; watch out for her!

If you find this bitter one you can have my soul for dessert.
If she's in the Underworld, then that's the place to go.

She's a night-woman, shameless, disreputable, and red.
If you find her, please bring her to Hafez's house.

THE SPIRIT WILL NEVER BE AT HOME

The Garden

HAFEZ

The garden is breathing out the air of Paradise today,
Toward me, a friend with a sweet nature, and this wine.

It's all right for the beggar to brag that he is a King today.
His royal tent is a shadow thrown by a cloud; his throne
    room is a sown field.

This meadow is composing a tale of a spring day in May;
The serious man lets the future go and accepts the cash now.

Do you really believe your enemy will be faithful to you?
The candle the hermit lights goes out in the worldly church.

Make your soul strong then by feeding it the secret wine.
When we have turned to dust, this rotten world will press
    our dust into bricks.

My life is a black book. But don't rebuke me too much.
No person can ever read the words written on his own
    forehead.

When Hafez's coffin comes by, it'll be all right to follow
    behind.
Although he is a captive of sin, he is on his way to the
    Garden.

The Grace of the Teacher

HAFEZ

Last night I walked sleep-stained to the door of the tavern.
My prayer rug and my patched cloak were stained with wine.

A young Zoroastrian boy stepped tauntingly from the door;
"Wanderer, wake up!" he said, "the way you walk has the
stain of sleep."

Our place is a tavern of ruin, so wash in clear water,
So that you will not leave stains on this holy house.

You are yearning for sweet lips; but those ruby tears you
weep
Stain your spirit. How long will this go on?

The way-station of old age is one to pass cleanly;
Don't let the urgencies of youth stain the whiteness of your
hair.

The great lovers have found their way into the deep ocean,
And drowned without ever taking one stain from the sea.

Become clean and pure; come up out of nature's well!
How could mud-stained water ever clean your face?

I said to the Great Soul: "Is there a problem then
If my book of roses in springtime is stained red with wine?"

The Soul replied: "Just cut out selling your friends these
subtle ideas."
"Hafez," I said, "the grace of the teacher is often stained
with rebukes."

The Pearl on the Ocean Floor

HAFEZ

We have turned the face of our dawn studies toward the
   drunkard's road.
The harvest of our prayers we've turned toward the granary
   of the ecstatic soul.

The fire toward which we have turned our face is so intense
It would set fire to the straw harvest of a hundred reasonable
   men.

The Sultan of Pre-Eternity gave us the casket of love's grief
   as a gift;
Therefore we have turned our sorrow toward this dilapi-
   dated traveller's cabin that we call "the world."

From now on I will leave no doors in my heart open for love
   of beautiful creatures;
I have turned and set the seal of divine lips on the door of
   this house.

It's time to turn away from make-believe under our robes
   patched so many times.
The foundation for our work is an intelligence that sees
   through all these games.

We have turned our face to the pearl lying on the ocean
   floor.
So why then should we worry if this wobbly old boat keeps
   going or not?

We turn to the intellectuals and call them parasites of reason;
Thank God they are like true lovers faithless and without
heart.

The Sufis have settled for a fantasy, and Hafez is no different.
How far out of reach our goals, and how weak our wills are!

THE SPIRIT WILL NEVER BE AT HOME

Joseph the lost will return
HAFEZ

Joseph the lost will return, Jacob should not sink into sadness;
Those who sit in the Grief House will eventually sit in the Garden.

The grieving chest will find honey; do not let the heart rot.
The manic hysterical head will find peace—do not sink into sadness.

If the way the Milky Way revolves ignores your desires
For two days, do not sink into sadness: All turning goes as it will.

I say to the bird: "As long as Spring baptizes the grass,
The immense scarlet blossoms will continue to sway over your head."

Even if the flood of materialism drowns everything,
Do not sink into sadness, because Noah is your captain.

Do not sink into sadness, even though the mysteries of the other world
Slip past you entirely. There are plays within plays that you cannot see.

Although the waystation you want to reach is dangerous and the goal
Distant, do not sink into sadness; all roads have an end.

We know our spiritual state: separated from God and punished by rivals.

Still do not sink into sadness. God is the one who changes
conditions.

Oh Hafez in the darkness of poverty and in the solitude of
the night,
As long as you can study and sing the Koran, do not sink into
sadness.

Translated by Robert Bly and Leonard Lewisohn

I am not I

JUAN RAMÓN JIMÉNEZ

I am not I.

        I am this one
Walking beside me whom I do not see,
Whom at times I manage to visit,
And whom at other times I forget;
The one who remains silent when I talk,
The one who forgives, sweet, when I hate,
The one who takes a walk where I am not,
The one who will remain standing when I die.

Oceans

JUAN RAMÓN JIMÉNEZ

I have a feeling that my boat
has struck, down there in the depths,
against a great thing.
             And nothing
happens! Nothing . . . Silence . . . Waves. . . .

   —Nothing happens? Or has everything happened,
and are we standing now, quietly, in the new life?

Conversation in the Mountains

LI PO

If you were to ask me why I dwell among green mountains,
I should laugh silently; my soul is serene.
The peach blossom follows the moving water;
There is another heaven and earth beyond the world of men.

Translated by Robert Payne

All the fruit

FRIEDRICH HÖLDERLIN

All the fruit is ripe, plunged in fire, cooked,
And they have passed their test on earth, and one law is this:
That everything curls inward, like snakes,
Prophetic, dreaming on
The hills of heaven. And many things
Have to stay on the shoulders like a load
of failure. However the roads
Are bad. For the chained elements,
Like horses, are going off to the side,
And the old
Laws of the earth. And a longing
For disintegration constantly comes. Many things however
Have to stay on the shoulders. Steadiness is essential.
Forwards, however, or backwards we will
Not look. Let us learn to live swaying
As in a rocking boat on the sea.

THE SPIRIT WILL NEVER BE AT HOME

from *Proverbs and Tiny Songs*

ANTONIO MACHADO

2

Why should we call
these accidental furrows roads? ...
Everyone who moves on walks
like Jesus, on the sea.

6

You walking, your footprints *are*
the road, and nothing else;
there is no road, walker,
you make the road by walking.
By walking you make the road,
and when you look backward,
you see the path that you
never will step on again.
Walker, there is no road,
only wind-trails in the sea.

7

I love Jesus, who said to us:
heaven and earth will pass away.
When heaven and earth have passed away,
my word will still remain.
What was your word, Jesus?
Love? Forgiveness? Affection?
All your words were
one word: Wakeup.

11

All things die and all things live forever;
but our task is to die,
to die making roads,
roads over the sea.

12

To die. . . . To fall like a drop
of sea water into the immense sea?
Or to be what I have never been:
one man, without shadow, without dream,
a man all alone, walking
with no road, with no mirror?

THE SPIRIT WILL NEVER BE AT HOME

Sssh

ROLF JACOBSEN

Sssh the sea says
Sssh the small waves at the shore say, sssh
Not so violent, not
So haughty, not
So remarkable.
Sssh
Say the tips of the waves
Crowding around the headland's
Surf. Sssh
They say to people
This is *our* earth,
Our eternity.

I find you in all these things of the world

RAINER MARIA RILKE

I find you in all these things of the world
that I love calmly, like a brother;
in things no one cares for, you brood like a seed;
and to powerful things you give an immense power.

Strength plays such a marvelous game—
it moves through the things of the world like a servant,
groping out in roots, tapering in trunks,
and in the treetops like a rising from the dead.

THE SPIRIT WILL NEVER BE AT HOME

Last Night, As I Was Sleeping

ANTONIO MACHADO

Last night, as I was sleeping,
I dreamt—marvellous error!—
that a spring was breaking
out in my heart.
I said: Along which secret aqueduct,
Oh water, are you coming to me,
water of a new life
that I have never drunk?

Last night, as I was sleeping,
I dreamt—marvellous error!—
that I had a beehive
here inside my heart.
And the golden bees
were making white combs
and sweet honey
from my old failures.

Last night, as I was sleeping,
I dreamt—marvellous error!—
that a fiery sun was giving
light inside my heart.
It was fiery because I felt
warmth as from a hearth,
and sun because it gave light
and brought tears to my eyes.

Last night, as I was sleeping,
I dreamt—marvellous error!—
that it was God I had
here inside my heart.

THE SPIRIT WILL NEVER BE AT HOME

Voyages II

HART CRANE

And yet this great wink of eternity,
Of rimless floods, unfettered leewardings,
Samite sheeted and processioned where
Her undinal vast belly moonward bends,
Laughing the wrapt inflections of our love;

Take this Sea, whose diapason knells
On scrolls of silver snowy sentences,
The sceptred terror of whose sessions rends
As her demeanors motion well or ill,
All but the pieties of lovers' hands.

And onward, as bells off San Salvador
Salute the crocus lustres of the stars,
In these poinsettia meadows of her tides,—
Adagios of islands, O my Prodigal,
Complete the dark confessions her veins spell.

Mark how her turning shoulders wind the hours,
And hasten while her penniless rich palms
Pass superscription of bent foam and wave,—
Hasten, while they are true,—sleep, death, desire,
Close round one instant in one floating flower.

Bind us in time, O Seasons clear, and awe.
O minstrel galleons of Carib fire,
Bequeath us to no earthly shore until
Is answered in the vortex of our grave
The seal's wide spindrift gaze toward paradise.

COPYRIGHT ACKNOWLEDGMENTS

Anonymous, "The Red Goddess" from *Hymn to Tirumal*, translated from the Tamil by A. K. Ramanujan from *Poems of Love and War: From the Eight Anthologies and the Ten Long Poems of the Tamil*. Copyright © 1985 by Columbia University Press. Reprinted with the permission of the publishers.

Apuleius, "Prayer to the Mother" from *The Golden Ass*, translated by Robert Graves. Copyright © 1951 by Robert Graves. Reprinted with the permission of Farrar, Straus & Giroux, Inc.

Farid al-Din Attar, "The Newborn" translated by Coleman Barks from *The Hand of Poetry: Five Mystic Poets of Persia* (New Lebanon, NY: Omega Publishers). Reprinted with the permission of Coleman Barks.

Hart Crane, "Voyages II" from *Complete Poems of Hart Crane*, edited by Marc Simon. Copyright © 1933, 1958, 1966 by Liveright Publishing Corporation. Copyright © 1986 by Marc Simon. Reprinted with the permission of Liveright Publishing Corporation.

Miguel de Guevara, "'Raise me up, Lord" from *Anthology of Mexican Poetry*, compiled by Octavio Paz, translated by Samuel Beckett. Copyright © 1958 by Indiana University Press. Reprinted with the permission of the publishers.

Emily Dickinson, "It is an honorable thought," "I'm ceded—I've stopped being Their's—," "Our journey had advanced," "Wild Nights—Wild Nights!," "We thirst at first—'tis Nature's Act," and

"I think the Hemlock likes to stand" from *The Complete Poems of Emily Dickinson*, edited by Thomas H. Johnson. Copyright © 1951, 1955 1979, 1983 by The President and Fellows of Harvard College. Reprinted with the permission of The Belknap Press of Harvard University Press.

The Countess of Die, "A Certain Knight" from *Songs of the Troubadours*, translated by Anthony Bonner. Copyright © 1972 by Anthony Bonner. Reprinted by permission.

H.D. (Hilda Doolittle), "The Mysteries Remain" from *Collected Poems 1912-1944*. Copyright © 1982 by The Estate of Hilda Doolittle. Reprinted with the permission of New Directions Publishing Corporation.

Ibn Faraj, "Chastity" from *Poems of Arab Andalusia*, translated by Cola Franzen from the Spanish version of Emilio Garcia Gomez. Copyright © 1989 by Cola Franzen. Reprinted with the permission of City Lights Books.

Johann Wolfgang von Goethe, "The Holy Longing" and "The Second Poem the Night-Walker Wrote" from *News of the Universe*, translated by Robert Bly. Copyright © 1980 by Robert Bly. Reprinted with the permission of Sierra Club Books.

Robert Graves, "To Juan at the Winter Solstice" from *Collected Poems 1975*. Copyright © 1975 by Robert Graves. Reprinted with the permission of Oxford University Press and Carcanet Press Limited.

Linda Gregg, "A Flower No More than Itself" from *The Sacraments of Desire* (Graywolf Press, St. Paul, Minn.). Copyright © 1991 by Linda Gregg. Reprinted with the permission of the author.

Hadewijch of Antwerp, "Love's Maturity" and "Knowing Love in Herself" from *Beguine Spirituality: Mystical Writings of Mechthild of Magdeburg, Beatrice of Nazareth, and Hadewijch of Antwerp*, edited by Fiona Bowie, translated by Oliver Davies (New York: Crossroad, 1989). Reprinted by permission.

Donald Hall, from "Praise for Death" from *Old and New Poems*. Copyright © 1990 by Donald Hall. Reprinted with the permission of the author and Ticknor & Fields/Houghton Mifflin Company.

Ibn Hazm, "Separation by Death" adapted by Robert Bly from the translation by Alois Richard Nykl, from *The Sea and Honeycomb*, edited by Robert Bly (Madison, Minn.: Sixties Press, 1966). Reprinted by permission.

Friedrich Hölderlin, "Bread and Wine, Part 7" and "All the Fruit" from *News of the Universe*, translated by Robert Bly. Copyright © 1980 by Robert Bly. Reprinted with the permission of Sierra Club Books.

Rolf Jacobsen, "Sssh" from *Twenty Poems by Rolf Jacobsen* (Madison, Minn.: Seventies Press, 1977). Reprinted by permission.

Kabir, all selections are from *The Kabir Book*, translated by Robert Bly. Copyright © 1971, 1977 by Robert Bly. Reprinted with the permission of Beacon Press and Macmillan Press Ltd.

Jane Kenyon, "Briefly It Enters, and Briefly Speaks" from *The Boat of Quiet Hours*. Copyright © 1986 by Jane Kenyon. Reprinted with the permission of Graywolf Press, St. Paul, Minn.

Babi Hayati Kermani, "Ghazal 96" translated from the Persian by Adam Harcani. Previously unpublished. Reprinted by permission.

COPYRIGHT ACKNOWLEDGMENTS

Galway Kinnell, "Daybreak" from *Mortal Acts, Mortal Words.* Copyright © 1980 by Galway Kinnell. Reprinted with the permission of Houghton Mifflin Company.

Lakshminkara, "'Lay your head on a block of butter and chop—" from *Passionate Enlightenment: Woman in Tantric Buddhism,* translated by Miranda Shaw. Copyright © 1994 by Princeton University Press. Reprinted with the permission of the publishers.

Lalla, all selections are from *Naked Song,* translated by Coleman Barks. Copyright © 1992 by Coleman Barks. Published by Maypop Books, Athens, GA. Reprinted with the permission of Coleman Barks.

Else Lasker-Schüler, "The Shulamite," translated from the German by Robert Alter. Poems from *Sämtliche Gedichte,* as found in *The Other Voice: Twentieth Century Women's Poetry in Translation,* edited by Joanna Bankier, Carol Cosman, Doris Earnshaw, Joan Keefe, Deirdre Lashgari, and Kathleen Weaver (New York: W. W. Norton & Company, 1976). Copyright © 1966 by Kösel-Verlag. Reprinted with the permission of the publishers.

Li Po, "Conversation in the Mountains" translated by Robert Payne from *The White Pony: An Anthology of Chinese Poetry from the Earliest Times to the Present Day.* Copyright 1947 by The John Day Company. Reprinted by permission.

Li Shang-Yin, "Written on a Monastery Wall" from *Poems of the Late Tang,* translated by A. C. Graham, Copyright © 1965 by A. C. Graham. Reprinted with the permission of Penguin Books, Ltd.

Hugh MacDiarmid, "A Herd of Does" from *Collected Poems 1920-1976, Volume I,* edited by Michael Grieve and William Aitken (London: Martin Brian & O'Keeffe, Ltd., 1978). Reprinted by permission of Carcanet Press Limited.

COPYRIGHT ACKNOWLEDGMENTS

Mahadeviyakka, "When Do I Join You?" translated from the Kannada by A. K. Ramanujan, from *Speaking of Siva*. Copyright © 1973 by A. K. Ramanujan. Reprinted with the permission of Penguin Books, Ltd.

Edna St. Vincent Millay, "Sonnet XII" of *Fatal Interview* from *Collected Poems* (New York: HarperCollins). Copyright © 1931, 1958 by Edna St. Vincent Millay and Norma Millay Ellis. Reprinted with the permission of Elizabeth Barnett, Literary Executor.

Mirabai, "O my friends," and "I was going to the river for water" translated from the Rajasthani by Jane Hirshfield from *Women in Praise of the Sacred* (New York: HarperCollins, 1994). Copyright © 1994 by Jane Hirshfield. Reprinted with the permission of the translator. "Ankle Bells," "The Clouds," "His Hair," "Don't go, don't go," "Where Did You Go?," "Faithfulness," "The Heat of Midnight Tears," "All I Was Doing Was Breathing," "It's True I Went to the Market," and "Why Mira Can't Go Back to Her Old House" translated from the Rajasthani by Robert Bly from *Mirabai: Versions*. Reprinted with the permission of Ken Botnick for Squid Ink, Penland, NC.

John G. Niehardt "White Buffalo Woman" from *Black Elk Speaks*. Copyright © 1932, 1959, 1972 by John G. Neihardt. Copyright © 1961 by the John G. Neihardt Trust. Reprinted with the permission of University of Nebraska Press.

Mary Oliver, "Maybe" from *New and Selected Poems*. Copyright © 1990 by Mary Oliver. Reprinted with the permission of the author and Beacon Press.

Owl Woman, "'How shall I begin my song'" from *Papago Music*, translated by Frances Densmore (New York: Da Capo Press, 1972). Reprint of Bulletin 90, Bureau of American Ethnology (Smithsonian Institute), 1929. Reprinted by permission.

COPYRIGHT ACKNOWLEDGMENTS

Kathleen Raine, "Loss of Memory" from *Collected Poems*. Reprinted with the permission of the author.

Rainer Maria Rilke, all selections are from *Selected Poems of Rainer Maria Rilke*, translated by Robert Bly. Copyright © 1981 by Robert Bly. Reprinted with the permission of HarperCollins Publishers, Inc.

Jelaluddin Rumi, "The Drunkards" translated by Robert Bly from *News of the Universe* by Robert Bly. Copyright © 1980 by Robert Bly. Reprinted with the permission of Sierra Club Books. "Eating Poetry," "Names," "The Edge of the Roof," "That Journeys are Safe," "The Mill, The Stone, and the Water," "The Hawk," and "The Jar With the Dry Rim" translated by Robert Bly from *When Grapes Turn To Wine: Versions of Rumi* (Cambridge, Mass.: Yellow Moon Press, 1986). Copyright © 1983 by Robert Bly. Reprinted by permission. "When Things Are Heard" translated by Robert Bly from *Night and Sleep* (Cambridge, Mass.: Yellow Moon Press, 1981). Reprinted by permission. "When I am with you, we stay up all night," "Love Dogs," "The Instruments," "Who Says Words With My Mouth," "Someone Digging in the Ground," "Say Yes Quickly," "I Have Such a Teacher," "I would love to kiss you," "Come to the orchard in the spring," "A Small Green Island," "Bread," "The Animal Soul," and "Sometimes I forget completely" translated by Coleman Barks from *The Essential Rumi* (San Francisco: HarperSanFrancisco, 1995). Reprinted with the permission of Coleman Barks. "The Force of Friendship," "On Resurrection Day," "The Snake-Catcher and the Frozen Snake," "Jesus on the lean donkey," and "Who makes these changes?" translated by Coleman Barks, from *This Longing: Poetry, Teaching Stories, and Letters of Rumi*, translated by Coleman Barks and John Moyne (Putney, VT: Threshold Books, 1988). Copyright © 1988. Reprinted with permission of Coleman Barks. "These spiritual windowshoppers," "A chickpea leaps almost over the rim of the pot" from *Rumi: We Are Three* translated by Coleman Barks (Putney, VT:

COPYRIGHT ACKNOWLEDGMENTS

Maypop, 1987). Copyright © 1987 by Coleman Barks. Reprinted with the permission of the translator.

Sappho, "To Aphrodite of the Flowers, at Knossos" from *Sappho: Lyrics in the Original Greek* translated by Willis Barnstone. Copyright © 1965 by Willis Barnstone. Reprinted by permission.

Edith Södergran, "There is no one" from *Love & Solitude: Selected Poems 1916-1923*, translated by Stina Katchadourian. Copyright © 1985 by Stina Katchadourian. Reprinted with the permission of Fjord Press.

William Stafford, "Roll Call" from *My Name Is William Tell* (Lewiston, ID: Confluence Press). Copyright © 1992 by William Stafford. Reprinted with the permission of Confluence Press of Lewis Clark State College, Lewiston, Idaho.

Wallace Stevens, "The Old Lutheran Bells at Home" from *The Collected Poems of Wallace Stevens*. Copyright 1954 by Wallace Stevens. Reprinted with the permission of Alfred A. Knopf, Inc.

Simone Weil, from *Random Thoughts on the Love of God*, translated from the French by Carol Cosman from *Pensées sans Ordre Concernant l'amour de Dieu*. Copyright by Editions Gallimard. Reprinted with the permission of the publisher.

W. B. Yeats, "A Voice" from *The Poems of W. B. Yeats: A New Edition*, edited by Richard J. Finneran. Copyright © 1940 by Georgie Yeats, renewed © 1968 by Bertha Georgie Yeats. Reprinted with the permission of Simon & Schuster, Inc.

261

INDEX

ABOUT THE EDITOR

Robert Bly is the author, editor, and translator of numerous works of poetry and prose. Among his most recent books are *Meditations on the Insatiable Soul* (poetry), *What Have I Ever Lost By Dying?* (prose poems), *Remembering James Wright* (a memoir), *American Poetry: Wildness and Domesticity* (essays about poetry), and *Iron John: A Book About Men*. He lives in Minnesota.